THE EMPERORS OF ROME AND BYZANTIUM

*Chronological and Genealogical
Tables for History Students
and Coin Collectors*

David R. Sear

London

British Library Cataloguing in Publication Data

Sear, David Ronald

The Emperor of Rome and Byzantium
1. Roman emperors – Tables
2. Byzantine emperors – Tables
I. Title
937'.06'0922   DG274

ISBN 0–900652–54–3

© Seaby Publications Ltd., 1974, 1981.
2nd Edition 1981
Reprinted 1987

Printed and bound in Great Britain
by R J Acford
Chichester Sussex
for the publishers
B.A. Seaby Ltd
8 Cavendish Square
London W1M 0AJ

Distributed by
B.T. Batsford Ltd
PO Box 4
Braintree Essex CM7 7QY

CONTENTS

PART I

THE ROMAN EMPIRE

INTRODUCTION

The idea of producing this book was first suggested to me by a coin collector almost ten years ago. His complaint was that none of the Seaby publications on Roman coins incorporated a chronological list of all the emperors, and that such lists in other works of reference were, at the best, somewhat incomplete, and at the worst, decidedly inaccurate. Since then other collectors have expressed similar views. Accordingly, I undertook the compilation of these lists, and hope that coin collectors and students of Roman history will find the results both interesting and useful.

The ancient sources of information for certain periods of Roman Imperial history, notably the Third Century, are very poor, and the evidence of the coins is of considerable value in a number of cases. For example, it is quite obvious, from the number of coins which he produced, that the Gallic usurper Marius reigned for a great deal longer than the two or three days with which he is credited by the author of the *Historia Augusta.* I have tried to maintain a balanced judgement in such cases, and to use my experience in Roman numismatics to reach the most likely conclusions. Happily, other periods are much better documented, and I have in the main followed such learned works as the *Cambridge Ancient History* and the *Cambridge Medieval History.*

One of the most serious short-comings of the Roman Imperial System was its failure to establish a satisfactory principle of succession to the throne. At the beginning, the imperial power, which was very much a personal creation of Augustus, was handed down through five generations of the same family. Thus, a dynastic system was established as the norm for the first century of the Empire's history. However, with Nero's suicide in A.D. 68 and the civil-wars which followed, it became clear that the army was going to have an important say in the selection of future emperors. The Senate cowered before the naked force of its martial rival, and braced itself to accept the unpleasant prospect of an absolute monarchy based on the power of the army. The inevitable chaos was temporarily postponed by a succession of strong and enlightened rulers who, throughout most of the Second Century, were able to hold at bay the relentless forces of destruction which were threatening the stability of the mighty Empire. Finally, however, after the fall of the Severan Dynasty in 235, the state of affairs quickly degenerated into military anarchy, with the provincial armies making and unmaking emperors at the slightest whim. On this occasion the ship of state came desperately close to foundering, and it took a man of great vision to put a stop to the rot, and set Roman history on a new course into calmer waters. This man, Diocletian, sought the means by which the imperial throne could be made more stable, and decided that henceforth the emperor should become a distant and remote figure to his subjects, closer to the oriental concept of divine monarchy. This was a far cry from the original Roman idea of the emperor as the "first citizen."

Diocletian's work was continued by his famous successor, Constantine, and during the latter's reign even the capital of the Empire was transferred from Rome to the eastern city of Byzantium, renamed Constantinople. The stage was now set for the disintegration of the western division of the Empire: within a century and a half of the foundation of Constantine's new capital, the former western provinces had become a patchwork of Teutonic kingdoms, whilst the eastern provinces looked forward to another thousand years of survival as the Byzantine Empire, a bridge between the classical civilizations of Antiquity and the Mediaeval World.

Having made this brief survey of the course of Roman history from the First to the Fifth Century, I can now proceed to less serious topics.

In a statistical work of this nature one is always tempted to produce sets of facts and figures which, though they are of little real value, never fail to amuse the reader. For example, the average Roman emperor ruled for just 6¼ years, and perished before reaching his forty-eighth birthday. This compares very unfavourably with our own English monarchy, where the average length of reign, from the time of Henry VII, is almost 21 years. It is often said that very few Roman emperors died in their beds, and this indictment is fully born out by the statistics. Only 31% died natural deaths, whilst the rest came to violent ends of a wonderfully varied nature: assassination, poisoning, suicide, death at the hands of the mob, and even one fascinating case of Jupiter losing his temper and striking down the unfortunate ruler with a flash of lightning.

For those interested in the regnal "top ten" of the Roman Empire, they are as follows:

1. Theodosius II, reigned for 48 years, 6 months, 18 days.
2. Augustus, reigned for 40 years, 7 months, 3 days.
3. Honorius, reigned for 30 years, 7 months, 15 days.
4. Constantine I, reigned for 30 years, 1 month, 22 days.
5. Valentinian III, reigned for 29 years, 4 months, 21 days.
6. Arcadius, reigned for 25 years, 3 months, 12 days.
7. Constantius II, reigned for 24 years, 1 month, 25 days.
8. Antoninus Pius, reigned for 22 years, 7 months, 25 days.
9. Tiberius, reigned for 22 years, 6 months, 25 days.
10. Hadrian, reigned for 20 years, 11 months, 2 days.

Finally, it is perhaps of some interest to note how infrequently a Roman emperor was actually succeeded by his own son. There are, in fact, only eleven instances of this occuring throughout the entire history of the Empire: Titus following Vespasian in A.D. 79; Commodus following Marcus Aurelius in 180; Caracalla and Geta following Severus in 211; Hostilian following Decius in 251; Gallienus following Valerian in 260; Carinus and Numerian following Carus in 283; Constantine following Constantius in 306; the three sons of Constantine succeeding him in 337; Gratian and Valentinian II following Valentinian I in 375; Arcadius and Honorius following Theodosius I in 395; and Theodosius II following Arcadius in 408. There is even one extraordinary case of a *father* succeeding a *son*, when the sickly child Leo II crowned his father Zeno co-emperor in 474.

INDEX

In the following lists an asterisk indicates that the emperor, empress or prince is not known to have issued coins (or to have had them struck in their honour).

A. EMPERORS.

B. EMPRESSES, etc.

d. = daughter; w. = wife; s. = sister; m. = mother.

Aelia Flaccilla, w. of THEODOSIUS I (101), m. of ARCADIUS (105) and HONORIUS (106).
*Aelia Paetina, w. of CLAUDIUS (4), m. of Claudia Antonia.
Agrippina Junior, d. of Germanicus, w. of CLAUDIUS (4), m. of NERO (5).
Agrippina Senior, d. of Agrippa, w. of Germanicus, m. of CALIGULA (3).
*Alypia. d. of ANTHEMIUS (122), w. of Ricimer.
*Anastasia, d. of CONSTANTIUS I (78), half-s. of CONSTANTINE I (87), m. of NEPOTIAN (93).
Annia Faustina, w. of ELAGABALUS (29).
Antonia, d. of Mark Antony, w. of Nero Claudius Drusus, m. of Germanicus and CLAUDIUS (4).
Aquilia Severa, w. of ELAGABALUS (29).
Ariadne, d. of LEO I (127), w. of ZENO (129), m. of LEO II (128).

*Baebiana, w. of TREBONIANUS GALLUS (44), m. of VOLUSIAN (45).

Caesonia, w. of CALIGULA (3).
Claudia, d. of NERO (5).
Claudia Antonia, d. of CLAUDIUS (4).
Constantia, d. of CONSTANTIUS I (78), half-s. of CONSTANTINE I (87), w. of LICINIUS (84).
*Constantia, d. of CONSTANTIUS II (90), w. of GRATIAN (99).
*Constantina, d. of CONSTANTINE I (87), w. of Hanniballianus.
Cornelia Supera, w. of AEMILIAN (46).
Crispina, w. of COMMODUS (19).

Didia Clara, d. of DIDIUS JULIANUS (21).
Domitia, w. of DOMITIAN (12).
Domitilla, w. of VESPASIAN (10), m. of TITUS (11) and DOMITIAN (12).
Domitilla, d. of VESPASIAN (10).
Drusilla, d. of Germanicus, s. of CALIGULA (3).
Dryantilla, w. of REGALIANUS (53).

Eudocia, w. of THEODOSIUS II (114), m. of Licinia Eudoxia.
Eudoxia, w. of ARCADIUS (105), m. of Pulcheria and THEODOSIUS II (114).
Euphemia, d. of MARCIAN (117), w. of ANTHEMIUS (122).

Fausta, d. of MAXIMIANUS (76), w. of CONSTANTINE I (87), s. of MAXENTIUS (82), m. of CONSTANTINE II (88), CONSTANTIUS II (90) and CONSTANS (89).
Faustina Junior, d. of ANTONINUS PIUS (16), w. of MARCUS AURELIUS (17), m. of Lucilla, COMMODUS (19) and Annius Verus.
Faustina Senior, w. of ANTONINUS PIUS (16), m. of Faustina Junior and Galerius Antoninus.

Galeria Valeria, d. of DIOCLETIAN (75), w. of GALERIUS MAXIMIANUS (79).
*Galla, d. of VALENTINIAN I (96), w. of THEODOSIUS I (101), s. of VALENTINIAN II (100), m. of Galla Placidia.
Galla Placidia, d. of THEODOSIUS I (101), w. of Ataulf and CONSTANTIUS III (113), half-s. of ARCADIUS (105) and HONORIUS (106), m. of Honoria and VALENTINIAN III (116).

Helena, w. of CONSTANTIUS I (78), m. of CONSTANTINE I (87).
*Helena, d. of CONSTANTINE I (87), w. of JULIAN II (94).
Herennia Etruscilla, w. of TRAJAN DECIUS (41), m. of HERENNIUS ETRUSCUS (42) and HOSTILIAN (43).
Honoria, d. of CONSTANTIUS III (113), s. of VALENTINIAN III (116).

Julia, d. of AUGUSTUS (1), w. of Agrippa and TIBERIUS (2), m. of Caius Caesar, Lucius Caesar, Agrippina Senior and Agrippa Postumus.
Julia, d. of TITUS (11).
Julia Domna, w. of SEPTIMIUS SEVERUS (24), s. of Julia Maesa, m. of CARACALLA (25) and GETA (26).
Julia Livilla, d. of Germanicus, s. of CALIGULA (3).
Julia Maesa, s. of Julia Domna, m. of Julia Soaemias and Julia Mamaea, grandm. of ELAGABALUS (29) and SEVERUS ALEXANDER (30).
Julia Mamaea, d. of Julia Maesa, m. of SEVERUS ALEXANDER (30).
Julia Paula, w. of ELAGABALUS (29).
Julia Soaemias, d. of Julia Maesa, m. of ELAGABALUS (29).
*Justina, widow of MAGNENTIUS (91), w. of VALENTINIAN I (96), m. of VALENTINIAN II (100) and Galla.

*Leontia, d. of LEO I (127), w. of Marcian (son of ANTHEMIUS).
Licinia Eudoxia, d. of THEODOSIUS II (114), w. of VALENTINIAN III (116) and PETRONIUS MAXIMUS (118).
Livia, w. of AUGUSTUS (1), m. of TIBERIUS (2) and Nero Claudius Drusus.
*Livilla, d. of Nero Claudius Drusus, s. of CLAUDIUS (4), w. of Drusus, m. of Tiberius Gemellus.
Lucilla, d. of MARCUS AURELIUS (17), w. of LUCIUS VERUS (18), s. of COMMODUS (19).

Magnia Urbica, w. of CARINUS (62), m. of Nigrinian (?).
Manlia Scantilla, w. of DIDIUS JULIANUS (21), m. of Didia Clara.
Marciana, s. of TRAJAN (14), m. of Matidia.
Mariniana, w. of VALERIAN (48), m. of GALLIENUS (49).
Matidia, d. of Marciana, niece of TRAJAN (14).
Messallina, w. of CLAUDIUS (4), m. of Octavia and Britannicus.
*Minervina, w. of CONSTANTINE I (87), m. of Crispus.

Octavia, s. of AUGUSTUS (1), w. of Mark Antony, m. of Antonia.
Octavia, d. of CLAUDIUS (4), w. of NERO (5).
Orbiana, w. of SEVERUS ALEXANDER (30).
Otacilia Severa, w. of PHILIP I (37), m. of PHILIP II (38).

Paulina, w. of MAXIMINUS I (31), m. of Maximus.
*Placidia, d. of VALENTINIAN III (116), w. of OLYBRIUS (123).
*Plautia Urgulanilla, w. of CLAUDIUS (4).
Plautilla, w. of CARACALLA (25).
Plotina, w. of TRAJAN (14).
Poppaea, w. of NERO (5), m. of Claudia.
Pulcheria, d. of ARCADIUS (105), w. of MARCIAN (117), s. of THEODOSIUS II (114).

Sabina, d. of Matidia, w. of HADRIAN (15).
Salonina, w. of GALLIENUS (49), m. of Valerian Junior and SALONINUS (50).
*Scribonia, w. of AUGUSTUS (1), m. of Julia.
*Severa, w. of VALENTINIAN I (96), m. of GRATIAN (99).
Severina, w. of AURELIAN (56).
Statilia Messallina, w. of NERO (5).

Theodora, step-d. of MAXIMIANUS (76), w. of CONSTANTIUS I (78).
Titiana, w. of PERTINAX (20), m. of Pertinax Caesar.
Tranquillina, w. of GORDIAN III (36).

Verina, w. of LEO I (127), m. of Ariadne and Leontia.
*Victoria, m. of VICTORINUS (68).
*Vipsania, w. of TIBERIUS (2), m. of Drusus.

ZENOBIA (71), *reigning empress* A.D. 271-2, m. of VABALATHUS (72).
Zenonis, w. of BASILISCUS (130), m. of MARCUS (131).

Nero Caesar, s. of Germanicus, br. of Drusus Caesar, CALIGULA (3), Agrippina Junior, Drusilla and Julia Livilla.
Nero Claudius Drusus, s. of Livia, br. of TIBERIUS (2), h. of Antonia, f. of Germanicus, Livilla and CLAUDIUS (4).
Nigrinian, s. of CARINUS ? (62).

*Orestes, f. of ROMULUS AUGUSTUS (126).

Pertinax Caesar, s. of PERTINAX (20).

Romulus, s. of MAXENTIUS (82).

Tetricus Junior, s. of, and Caesar under, TETRICUS (69).
*Tiberius Gemellus, s. of Drusus, grands. of TIBERIUS (2).
Trajan Pater, f. of TRAJAN (14).

Valerian Junior, s. of GALLIENUS (49), br. of SALONINUS (50), Caesar under his father and his grandfather VALERIAN (48).

C. PRINCES, etc.

s. = son; h. = husband; br. = brother; f. = father.

Aelius, Caesar under HADRIAN (15), f. of LUCIUS VERUS (18).
Agrippa, s.-in-law of AUGUSTUS (1), h. of Julia, f. of Caius Caesar, Lucius Caesar, Agrippina Senior and Agrippa Postumus.
Agrippa Postumus, s. of Agrippa, grands. of AUGUSTUS (1), br. of Caius Caesar, Lucius Caesar and Agrippina Senior.
Annius Verus, s. of MARCUS AURELIUS (17), br. of COMMODUS (19).
Antinous, favourite of HADRIAN (15).

Britannicus, s. of CLAUDIUS (4), br. of Octavia.

Caius Caesar, s. of Agrippa, grands. of AUGUSTUS (1), br of Lucius Caesar, Agrippina Senior and Agrippa Postumus.
Constantius Gallus, Caesar under CONSTANTIUS II (90), half-br. of JULIAN II (94).
Crispus, s. of, and Caesar under, CONSTANTINE I (87), half-br. of CONSTANTINE II (88), CONSTANTIUS II (90) and CONSTANS (89).

Decentius, br. of, and Caesar under, MAGNENTIUS (91).
Delmatius, grands. of CONSTANTIUS I (78), Caesar under CONSTANTINE I (87), br. of Hanniballianus.
Drusus, s. of TIBERIUS (2), h. of Livilla, f. of Tiberius Gemellus.
Drusus Caesar, s. of Germanicus, br. of Nero Caesar, CALIGULA (3), Agrippina Junior, Drusilla and Julia Livilla.

Galerius Antoninus, s. of ANTONINUS PIUS (16), br. of Faustina Junior.
Germanicus, s. of Nero Claudius Drusus, h. of Agrippina Senior, br. of Livilla and CLAUDIUS (4), f. of Nero Caesar, Drusus Caesar, CALIGULA (3), Agrippina Junior, Drusilla and Julia Livilla.

Hanniballianus, grands. of CONSTANTIUS I (78), Rex under CONSTANTINE I (87), br of Delmatius.

Julius Marinus, f. of PHILIP I (37).

Licinius Junior, s. of LICINIUS (84), Caesar under his father and under CONSTANTINE I (87).
Lucius Caesar, s. of Agrippa, grands. of AUGUSTUS (1), br. of Caius Caesar, Agrippina Senior and Agrippa Postumus.
Lucius Vitellius, f. of VITELLIUS (9).

*Marcian, s. of ANTHEMIUS (122), h. of Leontia.
Maximus, s. of, and Caesar under, MAXIMINUS I (31).

THE JULIO-CLAUDIAN DYNASTY

Emperor	Full Name	Born	Succeeded	Relationship to Predecessors	Died	Cause of Death, Age	Length of Reign	Relatives
1. AUGUSTUS	Caius Octavius, *later* Caius Julius Caesar.	23 Sept., 63 B.C., in Rome.	*Proclaimed Augustus* 16 Jan., 27 B.C., but was master of the Roman World from the defeat of Antony and Cleopatra in 31 B.C.	Great-nephew and adopted son of Julius Caesar (assassinated 44 B.C.)	19 Aug., A.D. 14, at Nola in Campania.	Natural causes, aged 75.	40 years, 7 months, 3 days.	*Wife:* 1. Scribonia, *divorced* 38 B.C. 2. Livia (Julia), *b.* 58 B.C., *m.* 38 B.C., *d.* A.D. 29. *Daughter:* Julia (by Scribonia), *b.* 39 B.C., *d.* A.D. 14. *Son-in-law:* M. Vipsanius Agrippa, *b.* 63 B.C., *m.* 21 B.C., *d.* 12 B.C. *Grandsons:* Caius Caesar, *b.* 20 B.C., *d.* A.D. 4. Lucius Caesar, *b.* 17 B.C., *d.* A.D. 2. Agrippa Postumus, *b.* 12 B.C., *d.* A.D. 14. *Sister:* Octavia, *b. circa* 64 B.C., *d. circa* 11 B.C.
2. TIBERIUS	Tiberius Claudius Nero, *later* Tiberius Julius Caesar.	42 B.C.	19 Aug., A.D. 14 [Had been heir-apparent from A.D. 4].	Stepson of Augustus (son of Tiberius Claudius Nero, praetor in 42 B.C., and Livia).	16 March, A.D. 37, at Misenum, in the villa of Lucullus.	Natural causes, aged 78	22 years, 6 months, 25 days.	*Wife:* 1. Vipsania Agrippina, *divorced* 11 B.C., *d.* A.D. 20 2. Julia (d. of Augustus), *m.* 11 B.C., *d.* A.D. 14. *Son:* Drusus (by Vipsania), *b.* 13 B.C., *d.* A.D. 23. *Grandson:* Tiberius Caesar (Gemellus), *b.* A.D. 19, *d.* A.D. 37. *Brother:* Nero Claudius Drusus, *b.* 38 B.C., *d.* 9 B.C. *Sister-in-law:* Antonia (d. of Mark Antony), *b.* 36 B.C., *m. circa* 16 B.C., *d.* A.D. 37. *Nephews:* Germanicus Caesar, *b.* 15 B.C., *d.* A.D. 19. Claudius, EMPEROR A.D. 41-54.
3. CALIGULA (A nickname meaning "little boot", given him in childhood by his father's soldiers).	Caius Caesar, *later* Caius Caesar Germanicus.	31 Aug., A.D. 12, at Antium.	16 March, A.D. 37.	Great-nephew of Tiberius; great-grandson of Augustus.	24 Jan., A.D. 41, at the Palatine games in Rome.	Assassinated by a tribune of the guard, at the age of 28.	3 years, 10 months, 8 days.	*Wife:* Caesonia. *Father:* Germanicus Caesar, *b.* 15 B.C., *d.* A.D. 19. *Mother:* Agrippina Senior (d. of Agrippa and Julia), *b. circa* 14 B.C., *m. circa* A.D. 5, *d.* A.D. 33. *Brothers:* Nero Caesar, *b.* A.D. 6, *d.* A.D. 30. Drusus Caesar, *b.* A.D. 7, *d.* A.D. 33. *Sisters:* Agrippina Junior, *b.* A.D. 15, *d.* A.D. 59. Drusilla, *b.* A.D. 17, *d.* A.D. 38. Julia Livilla, *b.* A.D. 18, *d.* A.D. 41.
4. CLAUDIUS	Tiberius Claudius Drusus, *later* Tiberius Claudius Drusus Germanicus.	1 Aug., 10 B.C., at Lugdunum.	25 Jan., A.D. 41.	Uncle of Caligula; nephew of Tiberius.	13 Oct., A.D. 54.	Probably poisoned by his wife Agrippina Junior, at the age of 63.	13 years, 8 months, 18 days.	*Wife:* 1. Plautia Urgulanilla. 2. Aelia Paetina. 3. Valeria Messallina, *m. circa* A.D. 39, *d.* A.D. 47. 4. Agrippina Junior, *m.* A.D. 48, *d.* A.D. 59. *Children:* Claudia Antonia (by Paetina), *b.* A.D. 27, *d.* A.D. 66. Octavia (by Messallina), *b. circa* A.D. 40., *d.* A.D. 62. Britannicus Caesar (by Messallina), *b. circa* A.D. 42, *d.* A.D. 55. *Father:* Nero Claudius Drusus, *b.* 38 B.C., *d.* 9 B.C. *Mother:* Antonia (d. of Mark Antony), *b.* 36 B.C., *m. circa* 16 B.C., *d.* A.D. 37. *Brother:* Germanicus Caesar, *b.* 15 B.C., *d.* A.D. 19.

Emperor	Full Name	Born	Succeeded	Relationship to Predecessors	Died	Cause of Death, Age	Length of Reign	Relatives
5. NERO	Lucius Domitius Ahenobarbus, *later* Nero Claudius Caesar Drusus Germanicus.	15 Dec., A.D. 37, at Antium.	13 Oct., A.D. 54. [Had been heir-apparent from A.D. 50].	Stepson of Claudius; nephew of Caligula; great-great-grandson of Augustus.	9 June, A.D. 68.	Suicide, aged 30.	13 years, 7 months 27 days.	*Wife*: 1. Octavia (d. of Claudius), *m.* A.D. 53, divorced A.D. 62. 2. Poppaea Sabina, *m.* A.D. 62, *d.* A.D. 65. 3. Statilia Messallina, *m.* A.D. 66. *Daughter*: Claudia (by Poppaea), *b.* and *d.* A.D. 63. *Mother*: Agrippina Junior, *b.* A.D. 15, *d.* A.D. 59.
6. CLODIUS MACER	Lucius Clodius Macer.	?	(Rebelled against Nero, in North Africa, about April of A.D. 68).	None.	About October A.D. 68.	Having refused to acknowledge Galba as emperor, Macer was probably murdered at that emperor's instigation. Age unknown.	(Rebellion probably lasted about 6 months).	
7. GALBA	Servius Sulpicius Galba.	*Circa* 5 B.C.·	9 June, A.D. 68.	None.	15 Jan., A.D. 69.	Assassinated in the Forum in Rome, aged approximately 72.	7 months, 6 days.	
8. OTHO	Marcus Salvius Otho.	A.D. 32.	15 Jan., A.D. 69.	None (but his wife, Poppaea Sabina, left him for Nero, whom she married in A.D. 62.	17 April, A.D. 69.	Suicide, at Brixellum at the age of 36.	3 months, 2 days.	*Wife*: Poppaea Sabina, *d.* A.D. 65.
9. VITELLIUS	Aulus Vitellius	A.D. 15.	Proclaimed emperor in Germany on 2 Jan., A.D. 69, in opposition to Galba.	None.	20 Dec., A.D. 69.	Killed by the mob, in Rome, at the age of 54.	11 months, 18 days.	*Father*: Lucius Vitellius, three times consul, and Claudius' colleague as censor; *d.* A.D. 52. *Children*: a son and a daughter, whose portraits, without names, appear on the coinage.

THE FLAVIAN DYNASTY

Emperor	Full Name	Born	Succeeded	Relationship to Predecessors	Died	Cause of Death, Age	Length of Reign	Relatives
10. VESPASIAN	Titus Flavius Vespasianus	A.D. 9, at Reate.	Proclaimed emperor at Alexandria (Egypt) on 1 July, A.D. 69, in opposition to Vitellius.	None.	24 June, A.D. 79.	Natural causes, aged 70.	9 years, 11 months 23 days.	*Wife*: Flavia Domitilla, *m.* before A.D. 39, *d.* before her husband's accession. *Children*: Titus, EMPEROR A.D. 79-81. Domitilla, predeceased her father. Domitian, EMPEROR A.D. 81-96.
11. TITUS	Titus Flavius Vespasianus	30 Dec., A.D. 39.	24 June, A.D. 79. [Had been Caesar from A.D. 69].	Son of Vespasian.	13 Sept., A.D. 81.	Probably natural causes, though his brother Domitian was suspected of having hastened his death. Age 41.	2 years, 2 months 20 days.	*Daughter*: Julia Sabina, *b. circa* A.D. 65, *d. circa* A.D. 91.
12. DOMITIAN	Titus Flavius Domitianus.	24 Oct., A.D. 51.	13 Sept., A.D. 81. [Had been Caesar from A.D. 69].	Brother of Titus; son of Vespasian.	18 Sept., A.D. 96.	Assassinated as the result of a palace plot, in which his wife, Domitia, was involved. Age 44.	15 years and 5 days.	*Wife*: Domitia Longina, *d.* A.D. 150.

Vespasian

Titus

Domitian

THE ADOPTIVE EMPERORS

Emperor	Full Name	Born	Succeeded	Relationship to Predecessors	Died	Cause of Death, Age	Length of Reign	Relatives
13. NERVA	Marcus Cocceius Nerva.	8 Nov., A.D. 30, at Narnia	18 Sept., A.D. 96.	None, though distantly related by marriage to the Julio-Claudian house.	25 Jan., A.D. 98.	Natural causes, aged 67.	1 year, 4 months, 7 days.	
14. TRAJAN	Marcus Ulpius Traianus	A.D. 53, at Italica, in Spain.	25 Jan., A.D. 98. [Had been Caesar from A.D. 97].	None.	8 Aug., A.D. 117.	Natural causes, aged 64.	19 years, 6 months, 14 days.	*Father*: Trajan Pater, *d.* A.D. 100. *Wife*: Pompeia Plotina, *d.* A.D. 129. *Sister*: Marciana, *d.* A.D. 112. *Niece*: Matidia, d. of Marciana, *d.* A.D. 119.
15. HADRIAN	Publius Aelius Hadrianus.	24 Jan., A.D. 76, at Italica, in Spain.	8 Aug., A.D. 117.	Grandson of Trajan's aunt; also, married to Trajan's grand-niece Sabina.	10 July, A.D. 138, at Baiae.	Natural causes, aged 62.	20 years, 11 months, 2 days.	*Wife*: Sabina (d. of Matidia, and grand-niece of Trajan), *m.* A.D. 100, *d. circa* A.D. 136. *Adopted Sons*: Aelius (L. Ceionius Commodus), Caesar A.D. 136-8. Antoninus Pius, EMPEROR A.D. 138-161. *Favourite*: Antinous, *d.* A.D. 130.
16. ANTONINUS PIUS	Titus Aurelius Fulvus Boionius Arrius Antoninus.	19 Sept., A.D. 86, at Lanuvium.	10 July, A.D. 138. [Had been Caesar from 25 Feb., A.D. 138].	None.	7 March, A.D. 161, at Lorium.	Natural causes, aged 74.	22 years, 7 months, 25 days.	*Wife*: Annia Galeria Faustina (Senior), *d.* A.D. 141. *Son*: M. Galerius Antoninus, died very young. *Daughter*: Annia Galeria Faustina (Junior), *d.* A.D. 175. *Adopted Sons*: Marcus Aurelius, EMPEROR A.D. 161-180. Lucius Verus, EMPEROR A.D. 161-169.
17. MARCUS AURELIUS	Marcus Annius Verus, *later* Marcus Aelius Aurelius Verus.	26 April, A.D. 121.	7 March, A.D. 161. [Had been Caesar from A.D. 139].	Nephew of Faustina Senior, the wife of Antoninus Pius; also son-in-law of Antoninus.	17 March, A.D. 180, at Vindobona on the Danube frontier.	Natural causes, aged 58.	19 years and 10 days.	*Wife*: Annia Galeria Faustina Junior (d. of Antoninus Pius and Faustina Senior), *m.* A.D. 145, *d.* A.D. 175. *Sons*: Commodus, EMPEROR A.D. 177-192. Annius Verus, *b.* A.D. 163, *d.* A.D. 169. *Daughter*: Annia Lucilla, *b.* A.D. 149, *m.* to L. Verus A.D. 164, and to Pompeianus A.D. 169, *d.* A.D. 183. *Son-in-law and co-emperor*: Lucius Verus, EMPEROR A.D. 161-9.
18. LUCIUS VERUS	Lucius Ceionius Commodus, *later* Lucius Aelius Aurelius Commodus	15 Dec., A.D. 130.	7 March, A.D. 161, as co-emperor with Marcus Aurelius.	Son of Aelius (Caesar under Hadrian A.D. 136-8).	A.D. 169, very early in year.	Natural causes, aged 38.	Almost 8 years.	*Wife*: Annia Lucilla (d. of M. Aurelius and Faustina Junior), *m.* A.D. 164.
19. COMMODUS	Lucius Aelius Aurelius Commodus	31 Aug., A.D. 161, at Lanuvium.	Proclaimed emperor in A.D. 177, as co-emperor with his father, M. Aurelius. [Had been Caesar from A.D. 175].	Son of Marcus Aurelius; grandson of Antoninus Pius.	31 Dec., A.D. 192.	Assassinated as the result of a palace plot. Age 31.	Approx. 15 years.	*Wife*: Bruttia Crispina, *m.* A.D. 178, *d. circa* A.D. 183.

Emperor	Full Name	Born	Succeeded	Relationship to Predecessors	Died	Cause of Death, Age	Length of Reign	Relatives
20. PERTINAX	Publius Helvius Pertinax.	1 Aug., A.D. 126, in Liguria.	1 Jan., A.D. 193.	None.	28 March, A.D. 193.	Assassinated by a band of mutinous guards. Age 66.	2 months, 27 days.	*Wife*: Flavia Titiana. *Son*: Pertinax Caesar (put to death by Caracalla following Geta's assassination in A.D. 212).
21. DIDIUS JULIANUS	Marcus Didius Julianus *later* Marcus Didius Severus Julianus.	*Circa* A.D. 135.	28 March, A.D. 193.	None.	2 June, A.D. 193.	Condemned to death by the Senate, and executed in the palace. Age approx. 58.	2 months, 5 days.	*Wife*: Manlia Scantilla. *Daughter*: Didia Clara.
22. PESCENNIUS NIGER	Caius Pescennius Niger.	Date uncertain, but probably between A.D. 135 and 140.	Proclaimed emperor in Syria in April, A.D. 193, in opposition to Didius Julianus.	None.	Autumn, A.D. 194.	Killed whilst fleeing to Parthia following his defeat in battle against Septimius Severus. Age mid to late 50's.	Approx. 18 months.	
23. CLODIUS ALBINUS	Decimus Clodius Septimius Albinus.	Date uncertain, but probably between A.D. 140 and 150, at Hadrumetum in Africa.	Proclaimed emperor in Gaul in the autumn of A.D. 195, in opposition to Septimius Severus. [Had been Caesar under Severus from A.D. 193].	None.	19 Feb., A.D. 197.	Committed suicide following his defeat in battle against Septimius Severus. Age uncertain, probably early-50's.	Approx. 15 months.	

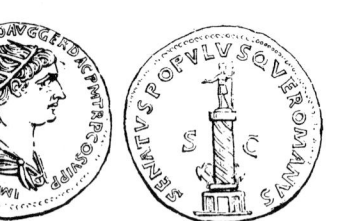

Trajan

Hadrian

Antoninus Pius

Lucius Verus

Pertinax

Didius Julianus

THE SEVERAN DYNASTY

Emperor	Full Name	Born	Succeeded	Relationship to Predecessors	Died	Cause of Death, Age	Length of Reign	Relatives
24. SEPTIMIUS SEVERUS	Lucius Septimius Severus.	A.D. 146 at Leptis Magna in Africa.	Proclaimed emperor 13 April, A.D. 193, at Carnuntum, in opposition to Didius Julianus.	None.	4 Feb., A.D. 211, at York.	Natural causes, aged 64.	17 years, 9 months, 22 days.	Wife: Julia Domna, d. A.D. 217. Sons: Caracalla, EMPEROR A.D. 198-217. Geta, EMPEROR A.D. 209-212.
25. CARACALLA (A nickname derived from a long tunic, of Gallic origin, which he adopted as his favourite dress).	Septimius Bassianus, later Marcus Aurelius Antoninus.	4 April, A.D. 186, at Lugdunum (Lyons).	Proclaimed emperor A.D. 198 (at beginning of year?), as co-emperor with his father, Septimius Severus. [Had been Caesar from A.D. 196].	Son of Septimius Severus.	8 April, A.D. 217, between Edessa and Carrhae.	Assassinated by an army officer. Age 31.	Approx. 19 years.	Wife: Plautilla (d. of the Praetorian Prefect Plautianus), m. A.D. 202, banished A.D. 205, d. A.D. 211. Brother: Geta, EMPEROR A.D. 209-212.
26. GETA	Lucius (later Publius) Septimius Geta.	27 May, A.D. 189, in Milan.	Proclaimed emperor Autumn A.D. 209, as co-emperor with his father, Septimius Severus, and brother, Caracalla. [Had been Caesar from A.D. 198].	Son of Septimius Severus; brother of Caracalla.	1 Feb., A.D. 212.	Assassinated in his mother's arms, at the instigation of his brother, Caracalla. Age 22.	Approx. 2¼ years.	
27. MACRINUS	Marcus Opellius Macrinus, later Marcus Opellius Severus Macrinus.	Circa A.D. 164, at Caesarea in Mauretania.	11 April, A.D. 217.	None.	June, A.D. 218, at Chalcedon.	Executed following defeat in battle against the forces of Elagabalus. Age approx. 54.	Approx. 14 months.	Son: Diadumenian, EMPEROR A.D. 218.
28. DIADUMENIAN	Marcus Opellius Diadumenianus, later Marcus Opellius Antoninus Diadumenianus.	Circa A.D. 208.	Proclaimed co-emperor with his father, Macrinus, shortly before the latter's defeat and death. [Had been Caesar from A.D. 217].	Son of Macrinus.	June, A.D. 218.	Put to death soon after his father's execution. Age approx. 10.	Unknown, but probably not more than a month and, possibly, much less.	

15

Emperor	Full Name	Born	Succeeded	Relationship to Predecessors	Died	Cause of Death, Age	Length of Reign	Relatives
29. ELAGABALUS (Named after the famous sun-god of Emesa of which he was the priest).	Varius Avitus, *later* Marcus Aurelius Antoninus.	A.D. 204, at Emesa.	Proclaimed emperor 16 May, A.D. 218, in opposition to Macrinus.	Second-cousin of Caracalla and Geta; great-nephew of Septimius Severus. (At the time of his rebellion against Macrinus, the rumour was spread that he was the illegitimate son of Caracalla: this was for propaganda purposes and was almost certainly untrue).	6 March, A.D. 222.	Assassinated in the praetorian camp. Age 17.	3 years, 9 months, 18 days.	*Grandmother*: Julia Maesa (sister of Julia Domna), *d. circa* A.D. 226. *Mother*: Julia Soaemias, *d.* A.D. 222. *Wife*: 1. Julia Cornelia Paula, *m.* A.D. 219. 2. Julia Aquilia Severa, *m.* A.D. 220. 3. Annia Faustina, *m.* A.D. 221. *Cousin*: Severus Alexander, EMPEROR A.D. 222-235.
30. SEVERUS ALEXANDER	Gessius Bassianus Alexianus, *later* Marcus Aurelius Severus Alexander.	1 Oct., A.D. 208, at Arca Caesarea in Phoenicia.	6 March, A.D. 222. [Had been Caesar from A.D. 221].	Cousin of Elagabalus; second-cousin of Caracalla and Geta; great-nephew of Septimius Severus.	Mid-March, A.D. 235, near Mainz.	Assassinated by mutinous troops. Age 26.	Approx. 13 years.	*Grandmother*: Julia Maesa (sister of Julia Domna), *d. circa* A.D. 226. *Mother*: Julia Mamaea, *d.* A.D. 235. *Wife*: Sallustia Barbia Orbiana, *m.* A.D. 225.

Elagabalus

Severus Alexander

Emperor	Full Name	Born	Succeeded	Relationship to Predecessors	Died	Cause of Death, Age	Length of Reign	Relatives
31. MAXIMINUS I	Caius Julius Verus Maximinus.	Of Thracian peasant stock, date of birth unknown.	Mid-March, A.D. 235.	None.	24 June, A.D. 238, at Aquileia.	Assassinated by mutinous troops. Age unknown.	Approx. 3¼ years.	Wife: Paulina (apparently died before her husband's accession). Son: Caius Julius Verus Maximus, Caesar A.D. 235-8.
32. GORDIAN I AFRICANUS	Marcus Antonius Gordianus.	Circa A.D. 157.	Proclaimed emperor in North Africa, on 22 March, A.D. 238, in opposition to Maximus.	None, though distantly related to Trajan on his mother's side.	12 April A.D. 238.	Committed suicide on hearing of his son's death in battle. Age approx. 80.	3 weeks.	Son: Gordian II Africanus, EMPEROR A.D. 238. Grandson: Gordian III, EMPEROR A.D. 238-44.
33. GORDIAN II AFRICANUS	Marcus Antonius Gordianus.	Circa A.D. 192.	Associated with his father, Gordian I, as co-emperor on 22 March, A.D. 238.	Son of Gordian I.	12 April, A.D. 238.	Killed in battle against Capellianus, governor of Numidia, who had remained loyal to Maximinus. Age approx. 45.	3 weeks.	Nephew: Gordian III, EMPEROR A.D. 238-44.
34. BALBINUS	Decimus Caelius Calvinus Balbinus.	Date of birth unknown.	Elected by the Senate, 22 April, A.D. 238, in succession to the Gordiáni and in opposition to Maximus.	None.	29 July, A.D. 238.	Assassinated by the Praetorians. Age unknown.	3 months, 7 days.	Adopted Heir: Gordian III, EMPEROR A.D. 238-44.
35. PUPIENUS	Marcus Clodius Pupienus Maximus	Date of birth unknown.	Elected by the Senate, 22 April, A.D. 238, as co-emperor with Balbinus.	None.	29 July, A.D. 238.	Assassinated by the Praetorians at the same time as Balbinus. Age unknown.	3 months, 7 days.	Adopted Heir: Gordian III, EMPEROR A.D. 238-44.
36. GORDIAN III	Marcus Antonius Gordianus.	Circa A.D. 225.	29 July, A.D. 238. [Had been Caesar from about May, A.D. 238].	Grandson of Gordian I, and nephew of Gordian II.	25 Feb., A.D. 244, near Zaitha.	Assassinated by his soldiers, at the instigation of the Praetorian Prefect, M. Julius Philippus. Age approx. 18.	5 years, 6 months, 27 days.	Wife: Furia Sabinia Tranquillina (d. of the Praetorian Prefect Timesitheus), m. A.D. 241.
37. PHILIP I	Marcus Julius Philippus	Circa A.D. 199.	25 Feb., A.D. 244.	None.	Sept., A.D. 249, near Verona.	Killed in battle against Decius. Age approx. 50.	5 years, 7 months (approx.)	Wife: Marcia Otacilia Severa. Son: Philip II, CO-EMPEROR A.D. 247-9. Father: Julius Marinus, d. before his son's accession.
38. PHILIP II	Marcus Julius Severus Philippus.	Circa A.D. 237.	Proclaimed emperor about May of A.D. 247, as co-emperor with his father. [Had been Caesar from A.D. 244].	Son of Philip I.	Sept., A.D. 249.	Either killed in battle at the same time as his father, or assassinated in the praetorian camp when news of the battle reached Rome. Age approx. 12.	2 years, 4 months (approx.)	

Emperor	Full Name	Born	Succeeded	Relationship to Predecessors	Died	Cause of Death, Age	Length of Reign	Relatives
39. PACATIAN	Tiberius Claudius Marinus Pacatianus.	Date of birth unknown.	Proclaimed emperor by the Danubian legions, in opposition to Philip, in the early summer of A.D. 248.	None.	Summer, A.D. 248.	Assassinated by his soldiers. Age unknown.	Very short, probably only several weeks.	
40. JOTAPIAN	Marcus Fulvius Rufus Iotapianus	Date of birth unknown.	Proclaimed emperor by the soldiers of Cappadocia in the summer of A.D. 248.	None (though he claimed a distant kinship with Severus Alexander).	Summer, A.D. 248.	Assassinated by his soldiers. Age unknown.	Very short, probably only several weeks.	
41. TRAJAN DECIUS	Caius Messius Quintus Decius, *later* Caius Messius Quintus Traianus Decius.	*Circa* A.D. 201, at Budalia in Lower Pannonia.	Sept., A.D. 249.	None.	June, A.D. 251, near Abrittus.	Killed in battle against the Goths. Age approx. 50.	1 year, 9 months (approx.)	*Wife*: Herennia Cupressenia Etruscilla. *Sons*: Herennius Etruscus, EMPEROR A.D. 251. Hostilian, EMPEROR A.D. 251.
42. HERENNIUS ETRUSCUS	Quintus Herennius Etruscus Messius Decius.	Date of birth unknown.	Proclaimed co-emperor with his father, Trajan Decius, in May, A.D. 251. [Had been Caesar from Sept., A.D. 250].	Son of Trajan Decius.	June, A.D. 251, near Abrittus.	Killed in battle against the Goths. Age unknown.	Approx. 1 month.	*Brother*: Hostilian, EMPEROR A.D. 251.
43. HOSTILIAN	Caius Valens Hostilianus Messius Quintus.	Date of birth unknown.	Proclaimed co-emperor by his father's successor, Trebonianus Gallus, about July, A.D. 251. [Had been Caesar from Dec., A.D. 250].	Son of Trajan Decius; Brother of Herennius Etruscus.	About Nov., A.D. 251.	Plague. Age unknown.	Approx. 4 months.	
44. TREBONIANUS GALLUS	Caius Vibius Trebonianus Gallus.	Date of birth unknown.	June, A.D. 251.	None.	Summer, A.D. 253, at Interamna, north of Rome.	Assassinated by his soldiers whilst advancing against Aemilian. Age unknown.	Approx. 2 years.	*Wife*: Afinia Gemina Baebiana. *Son*: Volusian, CO-EMPEROR, A.D. 251-3.
45. VOLUSIAN	Caius Vibius Afinius Gallus Vendumnianus Volusianus.	Date of birth unknown.	Proclaimed co-emperor with his father on the death of Hostilian, about Nov., A.D. 251. [Had been Caesar from about July A.D. 251].	Son of Trebonianus Gallus.	Summer, A.D. 253, at Interamna, north of Rome.	Assassinated with his father. Age unknown.	Approx. 19 months.	

Emperor	Full Name	Born	Succeeded	Relationship to Predecessors	Died	Cause of Death, Age	Length of Reign	Relatives
46. AEMILIAN	Marcus Aemilius Aemilianus	Date of birth unknown.	Proclaimed emperor by the soldiers of Moesia, summer A.D. 253, in opposition to Gallus and Volusian.	None.	Autumn, A.D. 253, near Spoletium.	Assassinated by his soldiers, whilst advancing against Valerian. Age unknown.	Approx. 3 months.	*Wife*: Cornelia Supera.
47. URANIUS ANTONINUS	Lucius Julius Aurelius Sulpicius Uranius Antoninus.	Date of birth unknown.	Proclaimed emperor A.D. 253 in order to organize the defence of Emesa against the Sassanid invader, Shapur.	None.	Presumably assassinated (or abdicated) on the arrival of Valerian in Syria in A.D. 254.	Unknown.	Probably less than 1 year.	
48. VALERIAN	Publius Licinius Valerianus.	*Circa* A.D. 193.	Proclaimed emperor by his troops in Raetia, about Sept., A.D. 253, in opposition to Aemilian	None.	Date of death unknown, but captured by Shapur of Persia about June, A.D. 260, and spent the remainder of his life in captivity.	Cause of death unknown. Age approx. 67 at the time of his capture.	6 years, 9 months. (approx.)	*Wife*: Mariniana, *d.* before her husband's accession. *Son*: Gallienus, EMPEROR A.D. 253-268. *Daughter-in-law*: Cornelia Salonina, *d.* A.D. 268. *Grandsons*: Publius Cornelius Licinius Valerianus (Valerian Junior), Caesar *circa* A.D. 256-8. Publius Licinius Cornelius Saloninus Valerianus, EMPEROR A.D. 259.
49. GALLIENUS	Publius Licinius Egnatius Gallienus	*Circa* A.D. 218.	Proclaimed co-emperor with his father Valerian, about Sept., A.D. 253.	Son of Valerian.	About Aug., A.D. 268.	Assassinated as the result of a conspiracy of his officers. Age approx. 50.	Almost 15 years.	*Wife*: Cornelia Salonina, *m. circa* A.D. 240, *d.* A.D. 268. *Sons*: Publius Cornelius Licinius Valerianus (Valerian Junior), Caesar *circa* A.D. 256-8. Publius Licinius Cornelius Saloninus Valerianus, EMPEROR A.D. 259.
50. SALONINUS	Publius Licinius Cornelius Saloninus Valerianus.	*Circa* A.D. 242.	Proclaimed emperor whilst being besieged in Cologne by Postumus, commander of the Rhine legions. A.D. 259. [Had been Caesar from A.D. 258].	Son of Gallienus; grandson of Valerian.	A.D. 259, at Cologne.	Executed by Postumus following the fall of Cologne. Age approx. 17.	Very short, probably only several weeks.	*Brother*: Publius Cornelius Licinius Valerianus (Valerian Junior), Caesar *circa* A.D. 256-8.

Emperor	Full Name	Born	Succeeded	Relationship to Predecessors	Died	Cause of Death, Age	Length of Reign	Relatives
51. MACRIANUS	Titus Fulvius Junius Macrianus.	Date of birth unknown.	Proclaimed emperor by his father, Macrianus (who was one of Valerian's officers) some time after that emperor's capture by the Persians — about Sept., A.D. 260.	None.	Spring, A.D. 261.	Killed in battle against Aureolus, one of Gallienus' generals. Age unknown.	Approx. 6 months.	*Father*: Macrianus Senior, killed in battle at the same time as his elder son. *Brother*: Quietus, EMPEROR A.D. 260-261.
52. QUIETUS	Titus Fulvius Junius Quietus.	Date of birth unknown.	Proclaimed emperor about Sept., A.D. 260, as co-emperor with his elder brother, Macrianus.	None.	About Nov., A.D. 261.	Executed by the inhabitants of Emesa whilst the city was being besieged by Odenathus, king of Palmyra. Age unknown.	Approx. 14 months.	*Father*: Macrianus Senior, killed in battle at the same time as his elder son. *Brother*: Macrianus, EMPEROR A.D. 260-261.
53. REGALIANUS	Publius Caius Regalianus.	Date of birth unknown.	Governor of Upper Pannonia when he was proclaimed emperor by his troops in the autumn of A.D. 260.	None. (but he claimed descent from Decebalus, the famous king of Dacia who was defeated by Trajan).	Autumn, A.D. 260.	Probably assassinated by his own soldiers at the approach of Gallienus' army. Age unknown.	Very short, probably only several weeks.	*Wife*: Sulpicia Dryantilla (d. of Sulpicius Pollio, an influential member of the Senate, and Claudia Ammiana Dryantilla).
54. CLAUDIUS II GOTHICUS	Marcus Aurelius Claudius.	May, A.D. 214, in Dardania (part of Moesia Superior).	About Aug., A.D. 268.	None.	Jan., A.D. 270, at Sirmium.	Plague. Age 55.	Approx. 17 months.	*Brother*: Quintillus, EMPEROR A.D. 270 (Some 40 years later, the Emperor Constantine claimed that his grandmother was a niece or daughter of Claudius Gothicus: the descent may not have been as direct as this, but it is unlikely that the claim was completely groundless.)
55. QUINTILLUS	Marcus Aurelius Claudius Quintillus.	Date of birth unknown, but he was the younger brother of Claudius.	Jan., A.D. 270.	Brother of Claudius Gothicus.	About April, A.D. 270.	Suicide. Age unknown.	Approx. 3 months.	
56. AURELIAN	Lucius Domitius Aurelianus.	*Circa* A.D. 207, at, or near, Sirmium.	About April, A.D. 270, having been declared emperor by his troops in opposition to Quintillus, who committed suicide shortly afterwards.	None.	**About** April, **A.D. 275.**	Assassinated as the result of a conspiracy of his officers. Age approx. 68.	Approx. 5 years.	*Wife*: Ulpia Severina (in whose name the government was carried on during the six-month interregnum between the death of her husband and the election of Tacitus.)

Emperor	Full Name	Born	Succeeded	Relationship to Predecessors	Died	Cause of Death, Age	Length of Reign	Relatives
57. TACITUS	Marcus Claudius Tacitus.	Circa A.D. 200.	Sept., A.D. 275: elected emperor by the Senate at the end of an interregnum which lasted almost six months, following the assassination of Aurelian.	None, (he did, however, claim descent from the great historian Tacitus, d. circa A.D. 120.)	About April, A.D. 276, at Tyana in Cappadocia.	Natural causes, aged approx. 76.	Approx. 7 months.	Half-brother: Florian, EMPEROR A.D. 276.
58. FLORIAN	Marcus Annius Florianus	Date of birth unknown.	About April, A.D. 276.	Half-brother of Tacitus.	End of June, A.D. 276, at Tarsus.	Assassinated by his own soldiers. Age unknown.	Approx. 2½ months	
59. PROBUS	Marcus Aurelius Probus.	Aug., A.D. 232, at Sirmium.	Proclaimed emperor by his troops late April or early May, A.D. 276, in opposition to Florian.	None.	Autumn, A.D. 282, at Sirmium.	Assassinated by a band of mutinous soldiers. Age 50.	6 years, 5 months (approx.)	
60. SATURNINUS	Sextus Julius Saturninus.	Date of birth unknown.	Rebelled against Probus at Alexandria (Egypt) in A.D. 280.	None.	A.D. 280 at Alexandria.	Assassinated by his own soldiers. Age unknown.	Probably very short as his coins are of the greatest rarity.	
61. CARUS	Marcus Aurelius Carus	Circa A.D. 230, possibly at Narona in Illyricum.	Proclaimed emperor by his troops in Raetia in the autumn of A.D. 282, shortly before Probus' assassination.	None.	About Aug., A.D. 283, near Ctesiphon, the Persian capital.	Officially, struck by lightning, but more probably a victim of the treachery of Arrius Aper, the Praetorian prefect. Age approx. 53.	Approx. 10 months.	Sons: Carinus, EMPEROR, A.D. 283-5. Numerian, EMPEROR, A.D. 283-4. Daughter-in-law: Magnia Urbica. Grandson (?): Nigrinian.
62. CARINUS	Marcus Aurelius Carinus.	Circa A.D. 249	About Aug., A.D. 283. [Had been Caesar from autumn of A.D. 282].	Son of Carus.	Spring, A.D. 285, in the valley of the Margus.	Assassinated by one of his own officers, whose wife he had seduced. Age approx. 35.	Approx. 20 months.	Wife: Magnia Urbica. Son: (?) Nigrinian (even if he was the son of Carinus, he seems to have been already dead by the time of his father's accession, as all his coins are posthumous). Brother: Numerian, CO-EMPEROR, A.D. 283-4.
63. NUMERIAN	Marcus Aurelius Numerianus.	Circa A.D. 254.	Proclaimed co-emperor with his brother Carinus, about Sept., A.D. 283. [Had been Caesar from late autumn of A.D. 282].	Brother of Carinus; son of Carus.	Nov., A.D. 284, whilst returning from the East.	Assassinated, probably by Arrius Aper, the Praetorian prefect. Age approx. 30.	Approx. 14 months.	

Emperor	Full Name	Born	Succeeded	Relationship to Predecessors	Died	Cause of Death, Age	Length of Reign	Relatives		
64. JULIAN of Pannonia.	Marcus Aurelius Julianus.	Date of birth unknown.	Rebelled against Carinus, in Pannonia, late in A.D. 284.	None.	Early in A.D. 285, near Verona.	Killed in battle against Carinus. Age unknown.	Very short, probably no more than 2 months.			

THE SECESSIONIST EMPIRES OF THE LATE THIRD CENTURY

Emperor	Full Name	Born	Succeeded	Relationship to Predecessors	Died	Cause of Death, Age	Length of Reign	Relatives
A. THE GALLIC EMPIRE								
65. POSTUMUS	Marcus Cassianius Latinius Postumus.	Date of birth unknown.	Rebelled against Gallienus, in Gaul, during A.D. 259.	None.	Late in A.D. 268, at Moguntiacum.	Assassinated by his own soldiers. Age unknown.	Approx. 9 years.	
66. LAELIANUS	Ulpius Cornelius Laelianus.	Date of birth unknown.	Rebelled against Postumus, summer, A.D. 268.	None.	Late in A.D. 268, at Moguntiacum.	Killed following the capture of Moguntiacum by Postumus. Age unknown.	Possibly about 4 months.	
67. MARIUS	Marcus Aurelius Marius.	Date of birth unknown.	Proclaimed emperor following the death of Postumus, late in A.D. 268.	None.	Early in A.D. 269.	Probably assassinated by his own soldiers. Age unknown.	Uncertain, but on the evidence of his coins probably about 2 months.	
68. VICTORINUS	Marcus Piavvonius Victorinus.	Date of birth unknown.	Proclaimed emperor following the death of Marius, early in A.D. 269.	None.	A.D. 270, at Cologne.	Assassinated by one of his own officers. Age unknown.	Uncertain; possibly about 18 months	*Mother*: Victoria, died during the reign of Tetricus.
69. TETRICUS	Caius Pius Esuvius Tetricus.	Date of birth unknown.	Proclaimed emperor following the death of Victorinus, A.D. 270.	Related in some way to Victoria and Victorinus, but the precise relationship is unknown.	Deposed by Aurelian, late in A.D. 273, pardoned, and given a post in the government of Southern Italy.	Presumably, natural causes. Date of death and age unknown.	Probably a little over 3 years.	*Son*: Caius Pius Esuvius Tetricus (Tetricus Junior), Caesar A.D. 270-73; also deposed and pardoned by Aurelian, and allowed to retire into private life.
70. DOMITIANUS	(This usurper is not mentioned by any of the historians of the period. His existence is known of only from a single coin found at Cleons, Loire Inferieure, in 1900, bearing the obverse inscription IMP. C. DOMITIANVS P.F. AVG. It is possible that he may be the same Domitianus who commanded the army which defeated the Macriani in A.D. 261. The style of his coin is obviously Gallic, and Domitianus might have made a momentary grasp at power in the troubled period following the assassination of Postumus.)							

Emperor	Full Name	Born	Succeeded	Relationship to Predecessors	Died	Cause of Death, Age	Length of Reign	Relatives
B. THE PALMYRENE EMPIRE								
71. ZENOBIA (Empress)	Septimia Zenobia	Date of birth unknown.	Became Queen of Palmyra on the assassination of her husband, Odenathus, in A.D. 267. Proclaimed Augusta, summer A.D. 271, in opposition to Aurelian.	Second wife of Odenathus, King of Palmyra (*dux* and *imperator* under Gallienus).	Deposed by Aurelian, summer, A.D. 272, and permitted to retire into private life.	Presumably, natural causes. Date of death, and age, unknown.	Augusta for about 1 year.	*Son*: Vabalathus (Athenodorus), EMPEROR A.D. 271-2.
72. VABALATHUS (ATHENODORUS)	Wahballat (Vabalathus or Vaballathus in Latin, Athenodorus in Greek).	Date of birth unknown, but was still very young at the time of Odenathus' assassination in A.D. 267.	Became King of Palmyra on the assassination of his father, Odenathus, in A.D. 267. Proclaimed Augustus summer, A.D. 271, in opposition to Aurelian.	Son of Odenathus, King of Palmyra (*dux* and *imperator* under Gallienus).	Deposed by Aurelian, summer A.D. 272. Subsequent fate unknown.	Unknown.	Augustus for about 1 year.	*Mother*: Zenobia, EMPRESS, A.D. 271-2.
C. THE BRITISH EMPIRE								
73. CARAUSIUS	Marcus Aurelius Mausaeus Carausius.	Date of birth unknown.	Commander of the Channel Fleet, he was proclaimed emperor late A.D. 286 or early 287, and ruled Britain and the northern coast of Gaul in opposition to the legitimate emperor Maximianus.	None.	A.D. 293.	Assassinated by his chief minister, Allectus. Age unknown.	Rather more than 6 years.	
74. ALLECTUS	(Unknown.)	Date of birth unknown.	A.D. 293, on the assassination of Carausius.	None.	A.D. 296.	Killed in battle against the Praetorian prefect Asclepiodotus, near Liss. Age unknown.	Approx. 3 years.	

THE JOVIAN AND HERCULIAN DYNASTIES, AND THE HOUSE OF CONSTANTINE

Emperor	Full Name	Born	Succeeded	Relationship to Predecessors	Died	Cause of Death, Age	Length of Reign	Relatives
75. DIOCLETIAN	Caius Aurelius Valerius Diocletianus.	*Circa* A.D. 245 in Dalmatia.	20 Nov., A.D. 284, following the death of Numerian.	None.	Abdicated 1 May, A.D. 305; died *circa* A.D. 316, at Split.	Natural causes, aged approx. 71.	20 years, 5 months, 11 days.	*Daughter*: Galeria Valeria, *m.* Galerius A.D. 293, *d. circa* A.D. 315.
76. MAXIMIANUS (First reign)	Marcus Aurelius Valerius Maximianus.	*Circa* A.D. 250, near Sirmium	Proclaimed emperor 1 April, A.D. 286, as co-emperor with Diocletian.	None.	Abdicated 1 May, A.D. 305.		19 years, 1 month.	*Son*: Maxentius, EMPEROR A.D. 306-12. *Step-daughter*: Flavia Maximiana Theodora, *m.* Constantius I A.D. 293. *Daughter*: Flavia Maxima Fausta, *m.* Constantine I A.D. 307, *d.* A.D. 326. *Grandsons*: Constantine II. EMPEROR A.D. 337-40. Constantius II, EMPEROR A.D. 337-61. Constans, EMPEROR A.D. 337-50. Romulus (s. of Maxentius), *d.* A.D. 309.
(Second reign)			Re-invested with the purple by his son, Maxentius, Nov., A.D. 306.		Forced to abdicate again, Nov., A.D. 308, at the Congress of Carnuntum.		Approx. 2 years.	
(Third reign)			Rebelled against Constantine, spring, A.D. 310, at Arles.		Spring, A.D. 310.	Committed suicide, or, more probably, executed on the orders of Constantine. Age approx. 60.	Very short, probably no more than a few weeks.	
77. DOMITIUS DOMITIANUS	Lucius Domitius Domitianus, *also known as* Achilleus.	Date of birth unknown.	Rebelled against Diocletian, at Alexandria (Egypt), *circa* July, A.D. 296.	None.	Early spring, A.D. 297, at Alexandria.	Executed by Diocletian. Age unknown.	Approx. 8 months.	
78. CONSTANTIUS I CHLORUS	Flavius Valerius Constantius	*Circa* A.D. 250, in Dardania (part of Moesia Superior).	1 May, A.D. 305. [Had been Caesar from 1 March, A.D. 293.)	Son-in-law of Maximianus. (He might also have been related to Claudius II Gothicus).	25 July, A.D. 306, at Eboracum (York).	Natural causes, aged approx. 56.	1 year, 2 months, 24 days.	*Wife*: 1. Flavia Julia Helena, *b. circa* A.D. 248, *divorced* A.D. 293, *d. circa* A.D. 328. 2. Flavia Maximiana Theodora (step-daughter of Maximianus), *m.* A.D. 293. *Son*: Constantine I (by Helena), EMPEROR A.D. 307-337. *Daughter*: Constantia (by Theodora), *m.* Licinius in A.D. 313, *d. circa* A.D. 330. *Grandsons*: Flavius Julius Crispus, Caesar A.D. 317-326. Constantine II, EMPEROR A.D. 337-40. Constantius II, EMPEROR A.D. 337-61. Constans, EMPEROR A.D. 337-50. Flavius Claudius Julius Constantius (Gallus), Caesar A.D. 351-4. Julian II, EMPEROR A.D. 360-63. Flavius Julius Delmatius, Caesar A.D. 335-7. Flavius Hanniballianus, Rex A.D. 335-7. Flavius Valerius Licinianus Licinius (Licinius Junior), Caesar A.D. 317-24. Nepotian, EMPEROR A.D. 350.

Emperor	Full Name	Born	Succeeded	Relationship to Predecessors	Died	Cause of Death, Age	Length of Reign	Relatives
79. GALERIUS MAXIMIANUS	Caius Galerius Valerius Maximianus.	Born near Serdica, date unknown.	1 May, A.D. 305. [Had been Caesar from 1 March, A.D. 293].	Son-in-law of Diocletian.	Beginning of May, A.D. 311.	Natural causes, age unknown.	6 years.	*Wife*: Galeria Valeria (d. of Diocletian), *m.* A.D. 293, *d.* circa A.D. 315. *Nephew*: Maximinus II, EMPEROR A.D. 309-13.
80. SEVERUS II	Flavius Valerius Severus.	Born in Pannonia, date unknown.	25 July, A.D. 306. [Had been Caesar from 1 May, A.D. 305].	None.	Summer, A.D. 307, having been deposed and imprisoned by Maximianus and Maxentius in the spring of the same year.	Executed, probably on the orders of Maxentius. Age unknown.	Approx. 8 months.	
81. MAXIMINUS II	Caius Galerius Valerius Maximinus, *originally called* Daia.	Date of birth unknown.	Assumed the rank of Augustus early in A.D. 309, not long after the Congress of Carnuntum. [Had been Caesar from 1 May, A.D. 305].	Nephew of Galerius.	Autumn, A.D. 313, at Tarsus.	Natural causes, age unknown.	Approx. 4¾ years.	
82. MAXENTIUS	Marcus Aurelius Valerius Maxentius.	Date of birth unknown.	Proclaimed emperor 28 Oct., A.D. 306, at Rome, in opposition to Severus II. [For a short period, prior to assuming the rank of Augustus, he used the titles "Princeps" and "Caesar"]	Son of Maximianus. Brother-in-law of Constantius Chlorus.	28 Oct., A.D. 312, at the Milvian Bridge, near Rome.	Killed in battle against Constantine. Age unknown.	6 years.	*Son*: Romulus, twice consul, died young in A.D. 309. *Sister*: Flavia Maxima Fausta, *m.* Constantine I A.D. 307, *d.* A.D. 326. *Half-sister*: Flavia Maximiana Theodora, *m.* Constantius I A.D. 293. *Brother-in-law*: Constantine I, EMPEROR A.D. 307-337.
83. ALEXANDER	Lucius Domitius Alexander.	Born in Phrygia, date unknown.	Rebelled against Maxentius, at Carthage, in A.D. 311.	None.	A.D. 311.	Either killed in battle against the Praetorian prefect C. Rufius Volusianus, or executed immediately after his defeat. Age unknown.	Uncertain, but probably quite short, as his coins are very rare.	

26

Emperor	Full Name	Born	Succeeded	Relationship to Predecessors	Died	Cause of Death, Age	Length of Reign	Relatives
84. LICINIUS	Valerius Licinianus Licinius.	*Circa* A.D. 263	Proclaimed emperor at the Congress of Carnuntum, Nov., A.D. 308, as colleague of Galerius.	None.	A.D. 325, having been deposed by Constantine, autumn, A.D. 324, and permitted to retire to Thessalonica.	Executed by Constantine following charges of attempted rebellion. Age approx. 62.	Almost 16 years.	*Wife*: Constantia (half-sister of Constantine), *m.* A.D. 313, *d. circa* A.D. 330. *Son*: Flavius Valerius Licinianus Licinius (Licinius Junior), Caesar A.D. 317-24. *Brother-in-law*: Constantine I, EMPEROR A.D. 307-337.
85. VALENS	Aurelius Valerius Valens	Date of birth unknown.	Proclaimed co-emperor by Licinius, autumn A.D. 314, during a civil war against Constantine.	None.	Late in A.D. 314, having been deposed following a truce between Constantine and Licinius.	Executed by Licinius. Age unknown.	Very short, probably only a few weeks.	
86. MARTINIAN	Marcus Martinianus.	Date of birth unknown.	Proclaimed co-emperor by Licinius, late summer, A.D. 324, during a civil war against Constantine.	None.	A.D. 325, having been deposed by Constantine, autumn, A.D. 324, and permitted to retire to Cappadocia.	Executed by Constantine, at the same time as Licinius. Age unknown.	Very short, probably only a few weeks	
87. CONSTANTINE I THE GREAT	Flavius Valerius Constantinus.	17 Feb., *circa* A.D. 274, at Naissus (Moesia).	Raised to the rank of Augustus by Maximianus, spring, A.D. 307, in Gaul.	Son of Constantius Chlorus. Son-in-law of Maximianus. (He also claimed kinship to Claudius II Gothicus).	22 May, A.D. 337, at Ancyrona, near Nicomedia.	Natural causes, aged approx. 63.	Just over 30 years.	*Mother*: Flavia Julia Helena, *b. circa* A.D. 248, *d. circa* A.D. 328. *Wife*: 1. Minervina. 2. Flavia Maxima Fausta (d. of Maximianus), *m.* A.D. 307, *d.* A.D. 326. *Sons*: Flavius Julius Crispus (by Minervina), Caesar A.D. 317-326. Constantine II (by Fausta), EMPEROR A.D. 337-40. Constantius II (by Fausta), EMPEROR A.D. 337-61. Constans (by Fausta), EMPEROR A.D. 337-50. *Daughters*: Constantina (by Fausta), *m.* Hanniballianus A.D. 335. Helena (by Fausta), *m.* Julian II A.D. 355, *d.* A.D. 360. *Half-sisters*: Constantia, *m.* Licinius A.D. 313, *d. circa* A.D. 330. Anastasia, mother of Nepotian, EMPEROR A.D. 350. *Nephews*: Flavius Claudius Julius Constantius (Gallus), Caesar A.D. 351-4. Julian II, EMPEROR A.D. 360-63. Flavius Julius Delmatius, Caesar A.D. 335-7. Flavius Hanniballianus, Rex A.D. 335-7. Flavius Valerius Licinianus Licinius (Licinius Junior), Caesar A.D. 317-24. Nepotian, EMPEROR A.D. 350.

Emperor	Full Name	Born	Succeeded	Relationship to Predecessors	Died	Cause of Death, Age	Length of Reign	Relatives
88. CONSTANTINE II	Flavius Claudius Constantinus.	A.D. 316, at Arles.	9 Sept., A.D. 337. [Had been Caesar from 1 March, A.D. 317]. Following Constantine I's death on 22 May, A.D. 337, there was an interregnum of over 3½ months, during which time the government was carried on in the dead emperor's name.	Son of Constantine I. Grandson of Constantius Chlorus and Maximianus. Nephew of Maxentius.	Spring, A.D. 340, near Aquileia	Killed in an ambush whilst advancing to attack his brother, Constans. Age 24.	Approx. 2½ years.	Brothers: Constantius II, EMPEROR A.D. 337-61. Constans, EMPEROR A.D. 337-50. Sisters: Constantina, m. Hanniballianus A.D. 335. Helena, m. Julian II A.D. 355, d. A.D. 360. Half-brother: Flavius Julius Crispus, Caesar A.D. 317-26. Cousins: Flavius Claudius Julius Constantius (Gallus), Caesar A.D. 351-4. Julian II, EMPEROR A.D. 360-63. Flavius Julius Delmatius, Caesar A.D. 335-7. Flavius Hanniballianus, Rex A.D. 335-7. Flavius Valerius Licinianus Licinius (Licinius Junior), Caesar A.D. 317-24. Nepotian, EMPEROR A.D. 350.
89. CONSTANS	Flavius Julius Constans	A.D. 320.	9 Sept., A.D. 337 [Had been Caesar from A.D. 333].	(Same as for Constantine II).	Early in A.D. 350, at the fortress of Helene, at the foot of the Pyrenees.	Assassinated by Gaiso, the barbarian emissary of the usurper Magnentius. Age 30.	Almost 12½ years.	Brothers: Constantine II, EMPEROR A.D. 337-40. Constantius II, EMPEROR A.D. 337-361. (otherwise same as for Constantine II).
90. CONSTANTIUS II	Flavius Julius Constantius.	7 Aug., A.D. 317, at Sirmium.	9 Sept., A.D. 337. [Had been Caesar from 8 Nov., A.D. 324].	(Same as for Constantine II and Constans).	3 Nov., A.D. 361, at Mopsucrenae in Cilicia.	Natural causes, aged 44.	24 years, 1 month, 25 days.	Brothers: Constantine II, EMPEROR A.D. 337-40. Constans, EMPEROR A.D. 337-50. (otherwise same as for Constantine II).
91. MAGNENTIUS	Flavius Magnus Magnentius.	Circa A.D. 303 of German descent.	Proclaimed emperor at Autun, 18 Jan., A.D. 350, in opposition to Constans.	None.	11 Aug., A.D. 353, at Lyons.	Suicide, aged approx. 50.	3 years, 6 months, 24 days.	Brother: Magnus Decentius, Caesar A.D. 351-3.
92. VETRANIO	(Unknown.)	Date of birth unknown.	Proclaimed emperor by the army of Illyricum on 1 March, A.D. 350.	None.	Abdicated late in A.D. 350 and pardoned by Constantius II, who allowed him to retire to Prusa in Bithynia. Died circa A.D. 356.	Natural causes, Age unknown.	Approx. 9 months.	

Emperor	Full Name	Born	Succeeded	Relationship to Predecessors	Died	Cause of Death, Age	Length of Reign	Relatives
93. NEPOTIAN	Flavius Julius Popilius Nepotianus Constantinus.	Date of birth unknown.	Proclaimed emperor by the Roman mob early in A.D. 350, in the troubled period following the revolt of Magnentius and the death of Constans.	Cousin of Constantine II, Constans and Constantius II; nephew of Constantine I; grandson of Constantius Chlorus.	Early in A.D. 350.	Murdered by the soldiers of Magnentius into whose hands he was betrayed. Age unknown.	28 days.	Cousins: Flavius Claudius Julius Constantius (Gallus), Caesar A.D. 351-4. Julian II, EMPEROR A.D. 360-63.

94. JULIAN II	Flavius Claudius Julianus.	April, A.D. 332, at Constantinople.	Proclaimed emperor by his troops at Paris, early in A.D. 360. [Had been Caesar from 6 Nov., A.D. 355].	Cousin of Constantine II, Constans, Constantius II and Nepotian; nephew of Constantine I; grandson of Constantius Chlorus.	26 June, A.D. 363, at Maranga in Persia.	Killed in battle against the Persians. Age 31.	Approx. 3¼ years.	*Wife*: Helena (d. of Constantine I and Fausta), m. A.D. 355, d. A.D. 360. *Half-brother*: Flavius Claudius Julius Constantius (Gallus), Caesar A.D. 351-4.
95. JOVIAN	Flavius Jovianus	*Circa* A.D. 331, at Singidunum (Belgrade).	27 June, A.D. 363.	None.	16 Feb., A.D. 364, at Dadastana in Galatia.	Suffocated through a brazier of charcoal having been left accidentally in his bedchamber. Age approx. 33.	7 months, 20 days.	

Constantius II

Magnentius

THE HOUSE OF VALENTINIAN AND THE THEODOSIAN DYNASTY

Emperor	Full Name	Born	Succeeded	Relationship to Predecessors	Died	Cause of Death, Age	Length of Reign	Relatives
96. VALENTINIAN I	Flavius Valentinianus.	A.D. 321, in Pannonia.	26 Feb., A.D. 364.	None.	17 Nov., A.D. 375, at Bregetio.	Natural causes, aged 54.	11 years, 8 months, 22 days.	*Wife*: 1. Valeria Severa, *divorced* A.D. 368. 2. Justina (widow of Magnentius), *m.* A.D. 368, *d.* A.D. 387. *Brother*: Valens, EMPEROR A.D. 364-78. *Sons*: Gratian (by Severa), EMPEROR A.D. 367-83. Valentinian II (by Justina), EMPEROR A.D. 375-92. *Great-grandson*: Valentinian III, EMPEROR A.D. 425-55.
97. VALENS	Flavius Valens.	A.D. 328, in Pannonia.	28 March, A.D. 364.	Brother of Valentinian I.	9 Aug., A.D. 378, near Hadrianopolis.	Killed in battle against the Goths. Age 50.	14 years, 4 months, 12 days.	*Nephews*: Gratian, EMPEROR A.D. 367-83. Valentinian II, EMPEROR A.D. 375-92.
98. PROCOPIUS	(Unknown.)	Date of birth unknown.	Rebelled against Valens, at Constantinople, 28 Sept., A.D. 365.	Related in some way to Julian II.	27 May, A.D. 366.	Executed, having been defeated by Valens. Age unknown	Almost 8 months.	
99. GRATIAN	Flavius Gratianus.	18 April, A.D. 359, at Sirmium.	Proclaimed Augustus 24 Aug., A.D. 367, as co-emperor with his father and uncle.	Son of Valentinian I; nephew of Valens.	25 May, A.D. 383, at Lyons.	Assassinated whilst fleeing from the usurper Magnus Maximus. Age 24.	16 years and 1 day.	*Wife*: Constantia (posthumous daughter of Constantius II), *b.* A.D. 362, *m.* A.D. 374, *d.* A.D. 383. *Half-brother*: Valentinian II, EMPEROR A.D. 375-92.
100. VALENTINIAN II	Flavius Valentinianus.	2 July, A.D. 371, at Acincum, in Pannonia, or, perhaps, at Treveri (Trier).	22 Nov., A.D. 375.	Son of Valentinian I; nephew of Valens; half-brother of Gratian.	15 May, A.D. 392, at Vienne.	Committed suicide, or, perhaps, assass-inated by order of his general Arbogast. Age 21.	16 years, 5 months, 23 days.	
101. THEODOSIUS I THE GREAT	Flavius Theodosius.	*Circa* A.D. 346, at Cauca, in Spain.	Proclaimed emperor by Gratian, 19 Jan., A.D. 379.	None.	17 Jan., A.D. 395, at Milan.	Natural causes, aged 49.	Almost 16 years.	*Wife*: 1. Aelia Flaccilla, *m. circa* A.D. 376, *d. circa* A.D. 386. 2. Galla (sister of Valentinian II), *m.* A.D. 388. *Sons*: Arcadius (by Flaccilla), EMPEROR A.D. 383-408. Honorius (by Flaccilla), EMPEROR A.D. 393-423. *Daughter*: Galla Placidia (by Galla), *b. circa* A.D. 388, *m.* Ataulf A.D. 414, and Constantius III A.D. 417, *d.* A.D. 450. *Grandsons*: Theodosius II, EMPEROR A.D. 402-50. Valentinian III, EMPEROR A.D. 425-55. *Grand-daughters*: Aelia Pulcheria (d. of Arcadius and Eudoxia), *b.* A.D. 399, *m.* Marcian A.D. 450, *d.* A.D. 453. Justa Grata Honoria (d. of Constantius III and Galla Placidia), *b.* A.D. 417, *d.* A.D. 454. *Great-grand-daughter*: Licinia Eudoxia (d. of Theodosius II and Eudocia), *b.* A.D. 422, *m.* Valentinian III A.D. 437, and Petronius Maximus A.D. 455.

Emperor	Full Name	Born	Succeeded	Relationship to Predecessors	Died	Cause of Death, Age	Length of Reign	Relatives
102. MAGNUS MAXIMUS	Magnus Clemens Maximus.	Date of birth unknown, but of Spanish origin.	Proclaimed emperor by his troops in Britain, July, A.D. 383, in opposition to Gratian.	None, though he did claim kinship with Theodosius.	28 July, A.D. 388, near Aquileia.	Executed following his defeat by Theodosius. Age unknown.	Approx. 5 years.	*Son:* Flavius Victor, EMPEROR A.D. 387-8.
103. FLAVIUS VICTOR	Flavius Victor.	Date of birth unknown.	Proclaimed co-emperor by his father, mid-A.D. 387.	Son of Magnus Maximus.	Aug., A.D. 388, in Gaul.	Executed by Arbogast, general of Theodosius, following his father's defeat and execution. Age unknown.	Approx. 1 year.	
104. EUGENIUS	(Unknown.)	Date of birth unknown.	Proclaimed emperor by Arbogast, 22 Aug., A.D. 392, after a three-month interregnum in the West following the death of Valentinian II.	None.	6 Sept., A.D. 394, between Aemona and Aquileia.	Executed, following his defeat by Theodosius. Age unknown.	2 years, 15 days.	
105. ARCADIUS	Flavius Arcadius.	A.D. 377.	Proclaimed co-emperor by his father, 19 Jan., A.D. 383.	Son of Theodosius I.	1 May, A.D. 408, at Constantinople.	Natural causes, aged 31.	25 years, 3 months, 12 days.	*Wife:* Aelia Eudoxia (d. of Bauto, the Frank), *m.* A.D. 395, *d.* A.D. 404. *Son:* Theodosius II, EMPEROR A.D. 402-50. *Daughter:* Aelia Pulcheria, *b.* A.D. 399, *m.* Marcian A.D. 450, *d.* A.D. 453. *Brother:* Honorius, EMPEROR A.D. 393-423. *Half-sister:* Galla Placidia, *b. circa* A.D. 388, *m.* Ataulf A.D. 414, and Constantius III A.D. 417, *d.* A.D. 450. *Grand-daughter:* Licinia Eudoxia, *b.* A.D. 422, *m.* Valentinian III A.D. 437, and Petronius Maximus A.D. 455.
106. HONORIUS	Flavius Honorius.	9 Sept., A.D. 384, at Constantinople.	Proclaimed co-emperor by his father, 10 Jan., A.D. 393.	Son of Theodosius I; brother of Arcadius.	25 Aug., A.D. 423, at Ravenna.	Natural causes, aged 39.	30 years, 7 months, 15 days.	*Brother:* Arcadius, EMPEROR A.D 383-408. *Half-sister:* Galla Placidia, *b. circa* A.D. 388, *m.* Ataulf A.D. 414, and Constantius III A.D. 417, *d.* A.D. 450. *Nephews:* Theodosius II, EMPEROR A.D. 402-50. Valentinian III, EMPEROR A.D. 425-55. *Nieces:* Aelia Pulcheria, *b.* A.D. 399, *m.* Marcian A.D. 450, *d.* A.D. 453. Justa Grata Honoria, *b.* A.D. 417, *d.* A.D. 454. *Brother-in-law:* Constantius III, EMPEROR A.D. 421.

Emperor	Full Name	Born	Succeeded	Relationship to Predecessors	Died	Cause of Death, Age	Length of Reign	Relatives
107. CONSTANTINE III	Flavius Claudius Constantinus.	Date of birth unknown.	Proclaimed emperor by the army in Britain, A.D. 407.	None.	Sept., A.D. 411.	Assassinated, at Honorius' command, whilst travelling as a prisoner to Ravenna following his capture by the general Constantius. Age unknown.	Approx. 4 years.	*Son*: Constans, EMPEROR A.D. 408-11.
108. CONSTANS	(Unknown.)	Date of birth unknown.	Proclaimed co-emperor by his father, A.D. 408.	Son of Constantine III.	Early A.D. 411, at Vienne.	Executed by the rebel general Gerontius. Age unknown.	A little over 2 years.	
109. MAXIMUS	(Unknown.)	Date of birth unknown.	Proclaimed emperor in Spain by the general Gerontius, A.D. 409, in opposition to the usurpers Constantine III and Constans.	None.	Deposed A.D. 411, and permitted by Honorius to retire into private life. Eventually put to death A.D. 422 at Ravenna.	Executed by Honorius as the result of an abortive rebellion *circa* A.D. 418. Age unknown.	Approx. 2 years.	
110. PRISCUS ATTALUS (First reign)	Priscus Attalus	Date of birth unknown.	Proclaimed emperor by the Roman Senate, A.D. 409, at the command of Alaric the Goth who was then besieging Rome.	None.	Deposed by Alaric, May or June, A.D. 410.		Approx. 1 year (?)	
(Second reign)			Re-invested with the purple by Ataulf, Alaric's successor, A.D. 414 (in Gaul).		Deposed again, A.D. 415, following the birth of a son to Ataulf and Placidia (Honorius' half-sister). Finally banished by Honorius to Lipara: date of death unknown.	Unknown.	Approx. 1 year. (?)	
111. JOVINUS	(Unknown.)	Date of birth unknown.	Proclaimed emperor by the Burgundian invaders of Gaul, A.D. 411.	None.	A.D. 413 at Narbonne.	Executed by order of Dardanus, Prefect of the Gauls; having been captured by Ataulf, who was in alliance with Honorius. Age unknown.	Approx. 2 years.	*Brother*: Sebastianus, EMPEROR A.D. 412-13.

Emperor	Full Name	Born	Succeeded	Relationship to Predecessors	Died	Cause of Death, Age	Length of Reign	Relatives
112. SEBASTIANUS	(Unknown.)	Date of birth unknown.	Proclaimed co-emperor by his brother, A.D. 412.	Brother of Jovinus.	A.D. 413.	Executed by Ataulf, who was in alliance with Honorius. Age unknown.	Probably less than 1 year.	
113. CONSTANTIUS III	Flavius Constantius.	At Naissus (Moesia), date unknown.	Proclaimed co-emperor by Honorius, 8 Feb., A.D. 421.	Brother-in-law of Honorius.	2 Sept., A.D. 421, at Ravenna.	Natural causes, age unknown.	Almost 7 months.	*Wife*: Galla Placidia (d. of Theodosius I), *b. circa* A.D. 388, *m.* A.D. 417, *d.* A.D. 450. *Son*: Valentinian III, EMPEROR A.D. 425-55. *Daughter*: Justa Grata Honoria, *b.* A.D. 417, *d.* A.D. 454.
114. THEODOSIUS II	Flavius Theodosius.	10 April, A.D. 401, at Constantinople.	Proclaimed co-emperor by his father, 10 Jan., A.D. 402.	Son of Arcadius; nephew of Honorius; grandson of Theodosius I.	28 July, A.D. 450, at Constantinople.	Natural causes (having injured his spine in a hunting accident). Age 49.	48 years, 6 months, 18 days.	*Wife*: Aelia Eudocia (originally named Athenais), *b.* A.D. 393, *m.* A.D. 421, *d.* A.D. 460. *Daughter*: Licinia Eudoxia, *b.* A.D. 422, *m.* Valentinian III A.D. 437, and Petronius Maximus A.D. 455. *Sister*: Aelia Pulcheria, *b.* A.D. 399, *m.* Marcian A.D. 450, *d.* A.D. 453. *Cousins*: Valentinian III, EMPEROR A.D. 425-55. Justa Grata Honoria, *b.* A.D. 417, *d.* A.D. 454.
115. JOHANNES	(Unknown.)	*Circa* A.D. 380.	25 Aug., A.D. 423, on the death of Honorius.	None.	Oct., A.D. 425.	Executed, following his defeat by an army sent by Theodosius II to champion the cause of the young Placidius Valentinianus. Age approx. 45.	A little over 2 years.	
116. VALENTINIAN III	Placidius Valentinianus.	2 July, A.D. 419, at Ravenna.	23 Oct., A.D. 425, following the fall of the usurper Johannes.	Son of Constantius III; nephew of Honorius; cousin of Theodosius II; grandson of Theodosius I; great-grandson of Valentinian I.	16 Mar., A.D. 455, at Rome.	Assassinated, in revenge for the murder of the great general Aetius, in the previous year. Age 36.	29 years, 4 months, 21 days.	*Mother*: Galla Placidia, *b. circa* A.D. 388, *m.* A.D. 417, *d.* A.D. 450. *Wife*: Licinia Eudoxia (d. of Theodosius II), *b.* A.D. 422, *m.* A.D. 437. *Daughter*: Placidia, *m.* Olybrius A.D. 462. *Sister*: Justa Grata Honoria, *b.* A.D. 417, *d.* A.D. 454. *Cousin*: Aelia Pulcheria, *b.* A.D. 399, *m.* Marcian A.D. 450, *d.* A.D. 453.
117. MARCIAN	Flavius Valerius Marcianus.	*Circa* A.D. 396, in Thrace.	25 Aug., A.D. 450, having been selected for the succession by Pulcheria, sister of Theodosius II.	None.	Jan. or Feb., A.D. 457.	Natural causes, aged approx. 61.	Approx. 6½ years.	*Wife*: 1. (name unknown.) 2. Aelia Pulcheria (sis. of Theodosius II), *b.* A.D. 399, *m.* A.D. 450, *d.* A.D. 453. *Daughter*: Aelia Marcia Euphemia (by his first wife), *m.* Procopius Anthemius.

THE FINAL COLLAPSE OF THE WESTERN EMPIRE

Emperor	Full Name	Born	Succeeded	Relationship to Predecessors	Died	Cause of Death, Age	Length of Reign	Relatives
118. PETRONIUS MAXIMUS	Flavius Anicius Petronius Maximus.	Circa A.D. 396.	17 Mar., A.D. 455.	None.	31 May, A.D. 455.	Killed by the mob in Rome, whilst fleeing from the approaching Vandal army. Age approx. 59.	2 months, 14 days.	*Wife:* Licinia Eudoxia (widow of Valentinian III).
119. AVITUS	Marcus Maecilius Flavius Eparchius Avitus.	In southern Gaul, date unknown.	Proclaimed emperor at Toulouse by the Visigoths, 9 July, A.D. 455.	None.	Deposed by the general Ricimer, 17 Oct., A.D. 456, and made bishop of Placentia. Died shortly afterwards.	Natural causes (?), age unknown.	year, 3 months, days.	
120. MAJORIAN	Julius Maiorianus.	Date of birth unknown.	1 April, A.D. 457 (more than 5 months after the fall of Avitus).	None.	Deposed by Ricimer, 2 Aug., A.D. 461. Died 7 Aug., at Tortona.	Executed by Ricimer, age unknown.	4 years, 4 months, 1 day.	
121. SEVERUS III	Libius Severus.	In Lucania, date unknown.	19 Nov., A.D. 461 (more than 3 months after the fall of Majorian).	None.	14 Nov., A.D. 465, at Rome.	Natural causes (?) age unknown.	Almost 4 years.	
122. ANTHEMIUS	Procopius Anthemius.	At Constantinople, date unknown.	12 April, A.D. 467 (almost 17 months after the death of Severus III).	Son-in-law of Marcian; also, descended from Procopius (A.D. 365-6).	11 July, A.D. 472, at Rome.	Executed by Ricimer, age unknown.	5 years, 2 months, 29 days.	*Wife:* Aelia Marcia Euphemia (d. of Marcian). *Daughter:* Alypia, m. Ricimer A.D. 467. *Son:* Marcian, m. Leontia (d. of Leo I and Verina).
123. OLYBRIUS	Anicius Olybrius.	Date of birth unknown.	Proclaimed emperor by Ricimer, April A.D. 472, in opposition to Anthemius.	None.	2 Nov., A.D. 472.	Natural causes, age unknown.	A little over 6 months.	*Wife:* Placidia (d. of Valentinian III), m. A.D. 462.
124. GLYCERIUS	Flavius Glycerius.	Date of birth unknown.	5 Mar., A.D. 473 (more than 4 months after the death of Olybrius).	None.	Deposed by Julius Nepos, 24 June, A.D. 474, and consecrated bishop of Salona. Date of death unknown.	Unknown.	1 year, 3 months, 19 days.	

Emperor	Full Name	Born	Succeeded	Relationship to Predecessors	Died	Cause of Death, Age	Length of Reign	Relatives
125. JULIUS NEPOS	Flavius Julius Nepos.	In Dalmatia, date unknown.	24 June, A.D. 474, having deposed his predecessor, Glycerius.	Related by marriage to the House of Leo.	Deposed by Orestes, the Master of Soldiers, and fled from Italy, 28 Aug., A.D. 475, to Dalmatia: remained there in exile until his murder, 9 May, A.D. 480.	Assassinated, age unknown.	1 year, 2 months, 4 days.	
126. ROMULUS AUGUSTUS	Romulus Augustus (*nicknamed* Augustulus).	Date of birth unknown, but very young at the time of his accession.	Proclaimed emperor by his father, Orestes, late Oct., A.D. 475, two months after the flight of Nepos.	None.	Deposed by Odovacar, the first barbarian King of Italy, late Aug., A.D. 476: permitted to retire to a Campanian villa; date of death unknown.	Unknown.	Approx. 10 months.	*Father*: Orestes, Master of Soldiers under Julius Nepos, executed by Odovacar 28 Aug., A.D. 476.

Emperor	Full Name	Born	Succeeded	Relationship to Predecessors	Died	Cause of Death, Age	Length of Reign	Relatives
127. LEO I	Flavius Valerius Leo.	*Circa* A.D. 411, in Thrace.	7 Feb., A.D. 457, following the death of Marcian.	None.	3 Feb., A.D. 474.	Natural causes, aged approx. 63.	Almost 17 years.	*Wife*: Aelia Verina, *d.* A.D. 484. *Daughters*: Aelia Ariadne, *m.* Zeno *circa* A.D. 467, and Anastasius I A.D. 491, *d.* A.D. 515. Leontia, *m.* Marcian (s. of Anthemius). *Grandson*: Leo II, EMPEROR A.D. 473-4. *Brother-in-law*: Basiliscus, EMPEROR A.D. 475-6.
128. LEO II	(Unknown.)	*Circa* A.D. 467.	Proclaimed co-emperor by his grandfather, 18 Nov., A.D. 473.	Grandson of Leo I.	10 Nov., A.D. 474.	Natural causes, aged approx. 7.	Almost 1 year (though on the evidence of the coins it would seem that he was relegated to the rank of Caesar in the latter part of A.D. 474).	*Father*: Zeno, EMPEROR A.D. 474-91. *Mother*: Ariadne, *d.* A.D. 515.
129. ZENO	Originally named Tarasicodissa, but changed this to Zeno, *circa* A.D. 467, on his marriage to Ariadne.	*Circa* A.D. 427, in Isauria.	Crowned co-emperor by his son, 9 Feb., A.D. 474.	Son-in-law of Leo I; father of Leo II.	9 April, A.D. 491. He was succeeded by Anastasius I, (A.D. 491-518), who is generally recognized as the first Byzantine emperor.	Natural causes, aged approx. 64.	17 years, 2 months.	*Wife*: Aelia Ariadne (d. of Leo I), *m. circa* A.D. 467, *d.* A.D. 515. *Son*: Leo II, EMPEROR A.D. 473-4. *Mother-in-law*: Aelia Verina, *d.* A.D. 484.
130. BASILISCUS	(Unknown.)	Date of birth unknown.	Proclaimed emperor in Constantinople, Jan., A.D. 475, following the flight of Zeno to Isauria.	Brother-in-law of Leo I.	Deposed by Zeno, Aug., A.D. 476, and exiled to Cappadocia where he died, A.D. 477.	Executed, age unknown.	Approx. 19 months.	*Sister*: Aelia Verina, *d.* A.D. 484. *Wife*: Aelia Zenonis, *d.* A.D. 477. *Son*: Marcus, CO-EMPEROR A.D. 476
131. MARCUS	(Unknown.)	Date of birth unknown.	Proclaimed co-emperor by his father, early in A.D. 476 (?).	Son of Basiliscus.	Deposed at the same time as his father, and exiled to Cappadocia where he died, A.D. 477.	Executed, age unknown.	Uncertain, but probably not more than about 6 months.	*Mother*: Aelia Zenonis, *d.* A.D. 477.
132. LEONTIUS	(Unknown.)	*Circa* A.D. 430, in Syria.	Crowned emperor by the Empress Verina at the instigation of the general Illus, 19 July, A.D. 484. The coronation of this rival to Zeno took place at Tarsus, and this was the second revolt against her son-in-law in which Verina was implicated.	None.	A.D. 488.	Executed by Zeno. Age approx. 58.	Approx. 4 years, though for most of this time he was shut up in the Isaurian fortress of Cherris, besieged by the forces of Zeno.	

THE JULIO-CLAUDIAN DYNASTY

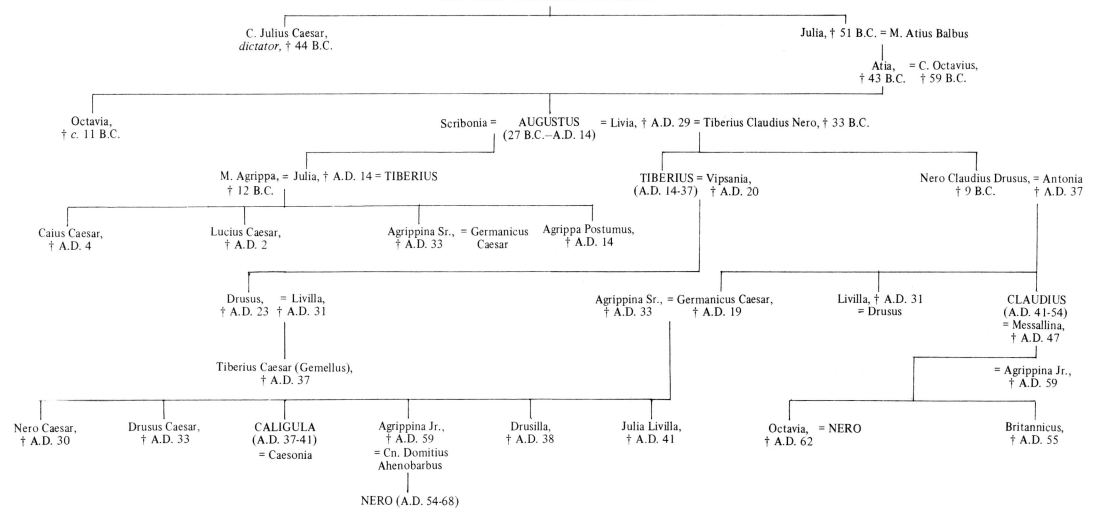

THE FLAVIAN DYNASTY

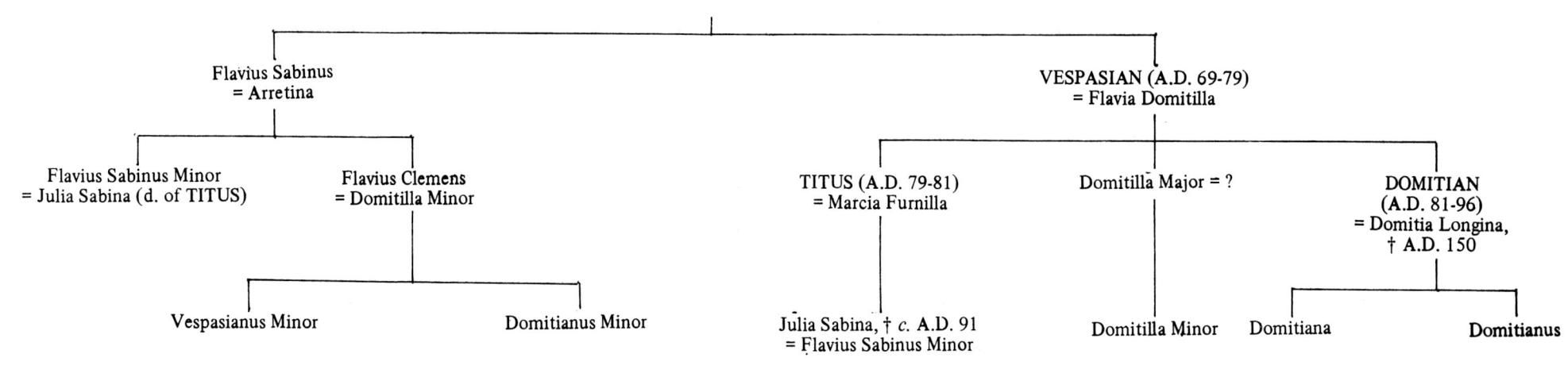

THE ANTONINE DYNASTY

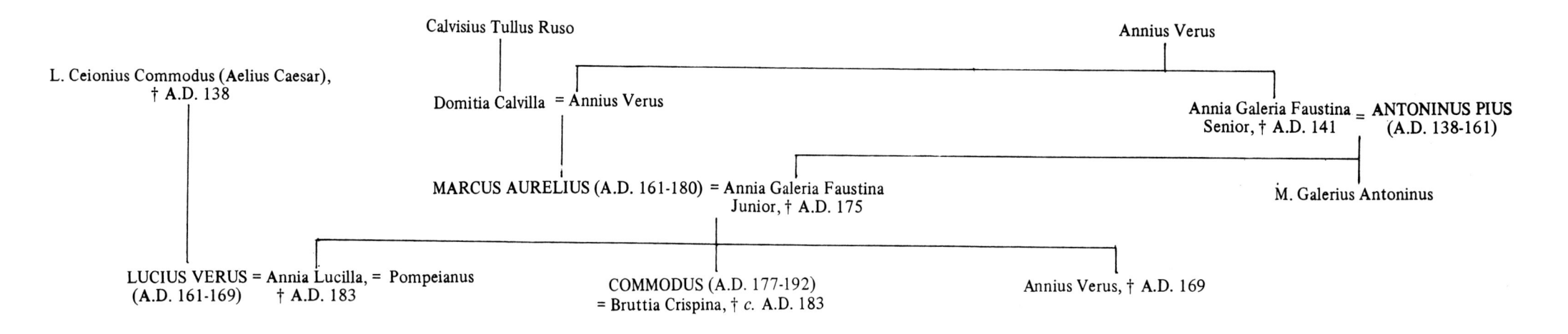

THE SEVERAN DYNASTY

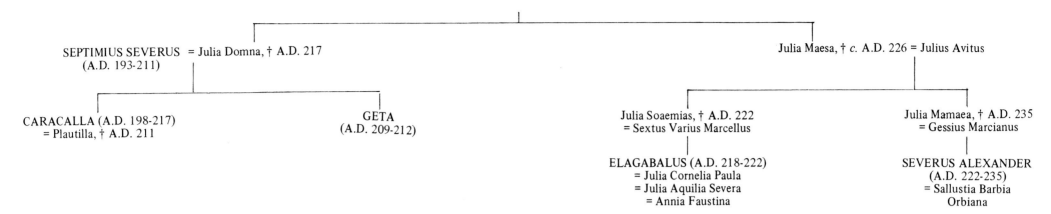

SEPTIMIUS SEVERUS = Julia Domna, † A.D. 217
(A.D. 193-211)

Julia Maesa, † *c.* A.D. 226 = Julius Avitus

CARACALLA (A.D. 198-217)
= Plautilla, † A.D. 211

GETA
(A.D. 209-212)

Julia Soaemias, † A.D. 222
= Sextus Varius Marcellus

Julia Mamaea, † A.D. 235
= Gessius Marcianus

ELAGABALUS (A.D. 218-222)
= Julia Cornelia Paula
= Julia Aquilia Severa
= Annia Faustina

SEVERUS ALEXANDER
(A.D. 222-235)
= Sallustia Barbia
Orbiana

THE HOUSE OF VALERIAN

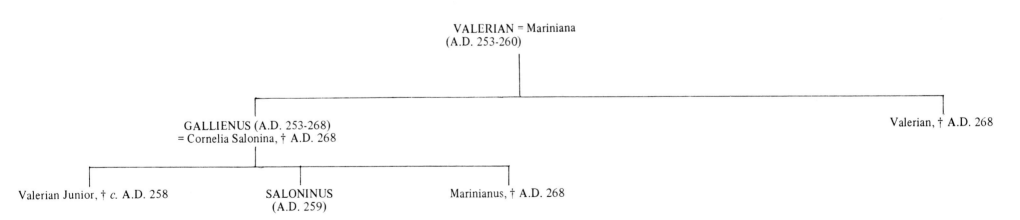

VALERIAN = Mariniana
(A.D. 253-260)

GALLIENUS (A.D. 253-268)
= Cornelia Salonina, † A.D. 268

Valerian, † A.D. 268

Valerian Junior, † *c.* A.D. 258

SALONINUS
(A.D. 259)

Marinianus, † A.D. 268

THE HOUSE OF CONSTANTINE

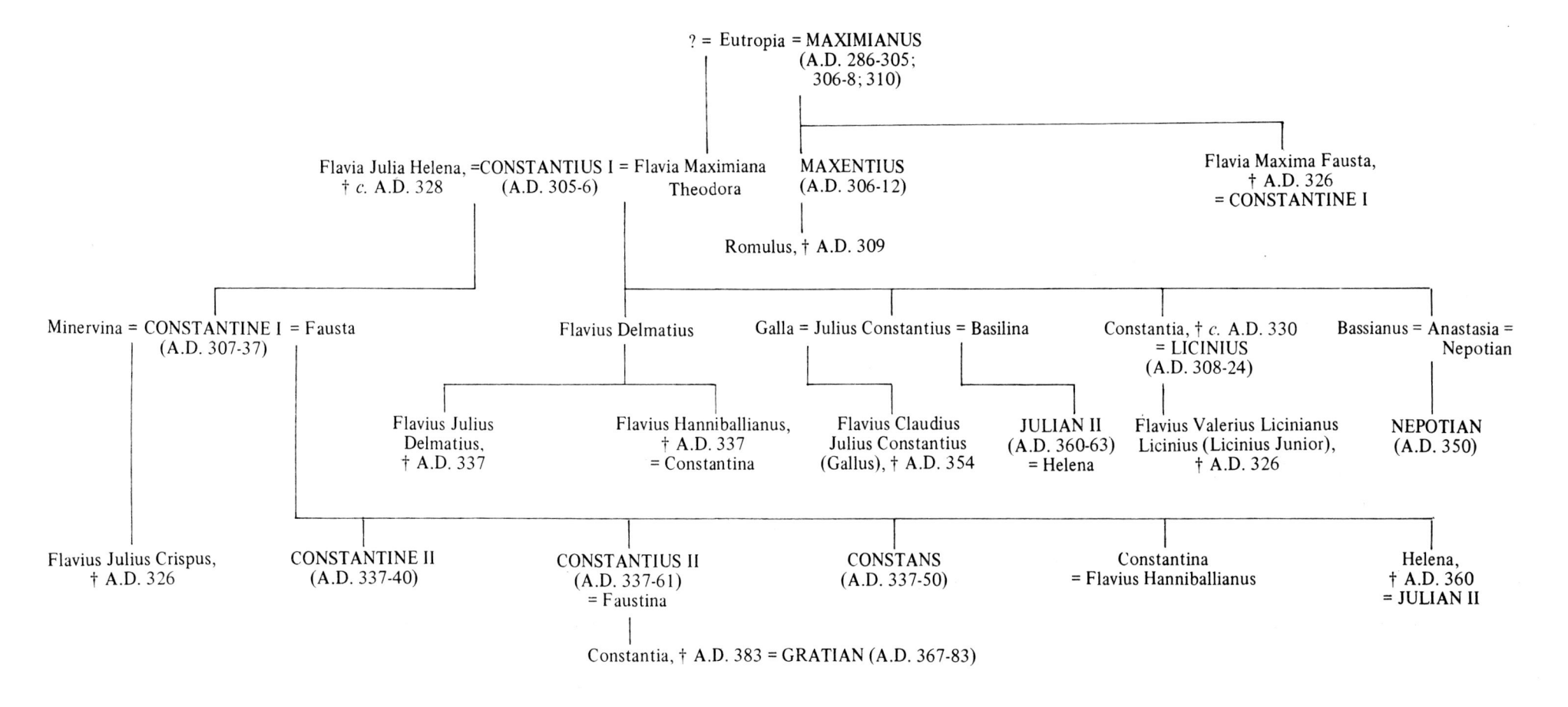

? = Eutropia = MAXIMIANUS
(A.D. 286-305;
306-8; 310)

Flavia Julia Helena, =CONSTANTIUS I = Flavia Maximiana   MAXENTIUS   Flavia Maxima Fausta,
† c. A.D. 328   (A.D. 305-6)   Theodora   (A.D. 306-12)   † A.D. 326
                                                                               = CONSTANTINE I

Romulus, † A.D. 309

Minervina = CONSTANTINE I = Fausta   Flavius Delmatius   Galla = Julius Constantius = Basilina   Constantia, † c. A.D. 330   Bassianus = Anastasia =
            (A.D. 307-37)   = LICINIUS   Nepotian
                                                                                                       (A.D. 308-24)

              Flavius Julius   Flavius Hanniballianus,   Flavius Claudius   JULIAN II   Flavius Valerius Licinianus   NEPOTIAN
              Delmatius,   † A.D. 337   Julius Constantius   (A.D. 360-63) Licinius (Licinius Junior),   (A.D. 350)
              † A.D. 337   = Constantina   (Gallus), † A.D. 354   = Helena   † A.D. 326

Flavius Julius Crispus,   CONSTANTINE II   CONSTANTIUS II   CONSTANS   Constantina   Helena,
† A.D. 326   (A.D. 337-40)   (A.D. 337-61)   (A.D. 337-50)   = Flavius Hanniballianus   † A.D. 360
                                             = Faustina   = JULIAN II

Constantia, † A.D. 383 = GRATIAN (A.D. 367-83)

THE HOUSE OF VALENTINIAN AND THE THEODOSIAN DYNASTY

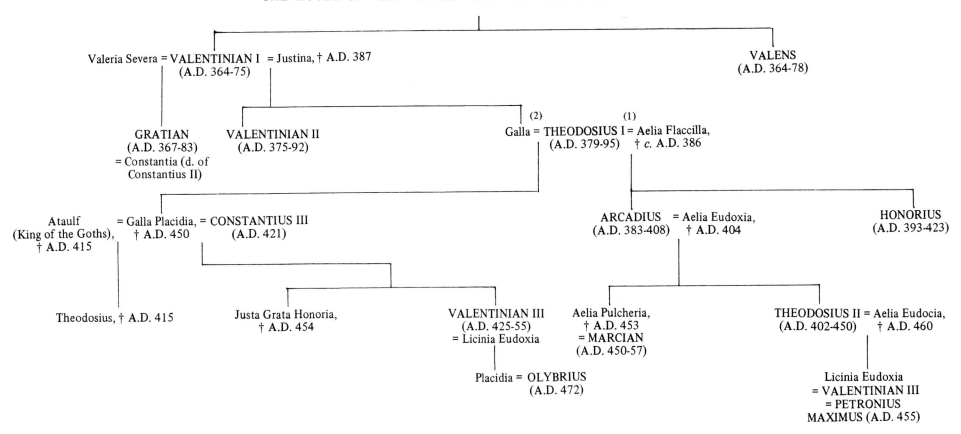

Valeria Severa = VALENTINIAN I = Justina, † A.D. 387
(A.D. 364-75)

VALENS
(A.D. 364-78)

GRATIAN
(A.D. 367-83)
= Constantia (d. of
Constantius II)

VALENTINIAN II
(A.D. 375-92)

(2)
Galla = THEODOSIUS I = Aelia Flaccilla,
(A.D. 379-95)   † c. A.D. 386
(1)

Ataulf
(King of the Goths),
† A.D. 415

= Galla Placidia, = CONSTANTIUS III
† A.D. 450   (A.D. 421)

ARCADIUS   = Aelia Eudoxia,
(A.D. 383-408)   † A.D. 404

HONORIUS
(A.D. 393-423)

Theodosius, † A.D. 415

Justa Grata Honoria,
† A.D. 454

VALENTINIAN III
(A.D. 425-55)
= Licinia Eudoxia

Aelia Pulcheria,
† A.D. 453
= MARCIAN
(A.D. 450-57)

THEODOSIUS II = Aelia Eudocia,
(A.D. 402-450)   † A.D. 460

Placidia = OLYBRIUS
(A.D. 472)

Licinia Eudoxia
= VALENTINIAN III
= PETRONIUS
MAXIMUS (A.D. 455)

THE HOUSE OF LEO

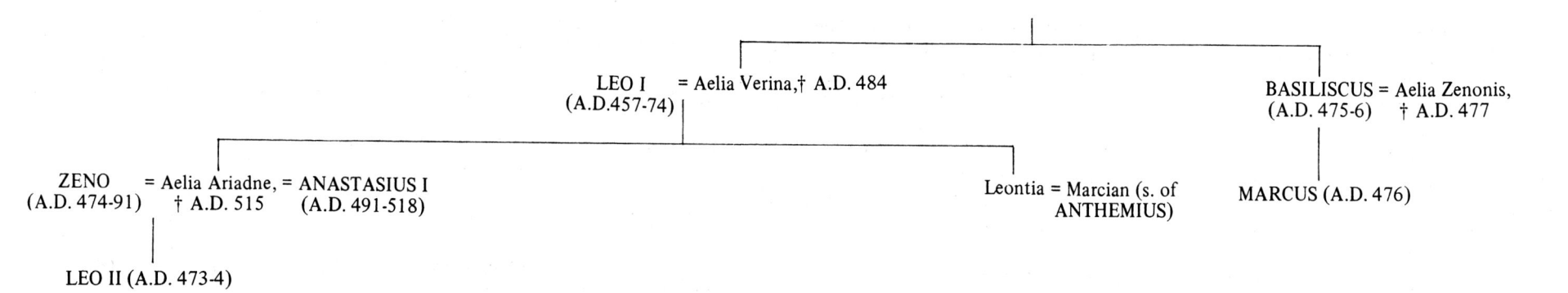

LEO I = Aelia Verina,† A.D. 484
(A.D.457-74)

BASILISCUS = Aelia Zenonis,
(A.D. 475-6)   † A.D. 477

ZENO   = Aelia Ariadne, = ANASTASIUS I
(A.D. 474-91)   † A.D. 515   (A.D. 491-518)

Leontia = Marcian (s. of
ANTHEMIUS)

MARCUS (A.D. 476)

LEO II (A.D. 473-4)

THE CHRONOLOGICAL SEQUENCE

OF THE ROMAN EMPERORS,

27 B.C. – A.D. 491

Augustus .... 27 B.C.-A.D. 14

Tiberius .... A.D. 14-37

Caligula .... A.D. 37-41

Claudius .... A.D. 41-54

Nero .... A.D. 54-68

Nero and Clodius Macer

        (usurper in N. Africa) A.D. 68

Galba and Clodius Macer .... A.D. 68

Galba .... A.D. 68-69

Galba and Vitellius .... A.D. 69

Otho and Vitellius .... A.D. 69

Vitellius .... A.D. 69

Vitellius and Vespasian .... A.D. 69

Vespasian .... A.D. 69-79

Titus .... A.D. 79-81

Domitian .... A.D. 81-96

Nerva . ... A.D. 96-98

Trajan ....A.D. 98-117

Hadrian .... A.D. 117-138

Antoninus Pius .... A.D. 138-161

Marcus Aurelius and Lucius Verus   A.D. 161-169

Marcus Aurelius .... A.D. 169-177

Marcus Aurelius and Commodus .... A.D. 177-180

Commodus .... A.D. 180-192

Pertinax .... A.D. 193

Didius Julianus .... A.D. 193

Didius Julianus, Pescennius Niger

        and Septimius Severus A.D. 193

Septimius Severus

        and Pescennius Niger A.D. 193-194

Septimius Severus .... A.D. 194-195

Septimius Severus

        and Clodius Albinus A.D. 195-197

Septimius Severus .... A.D. 197-198

Septimius Severus and Caracalla ..... A.D. 198-209

Septimius Severus, Caracalla and Geta A.D. 209-211

Caracalla and Geta .... A.D. 211-212

Caracalla .... A.D. 212-217

Macrinus .... A.D. 217-218

Macrinus and Diadumenian .... A.D. 218

Macrinus, Diadumenian and Elagabalus ..A.D. 218

Elagabalus .... A.D. 218-222

Severus Alexander .... A.D. 222-235

Maximinus I .... A.D. 235-238

Maximinus I, Gordian I and Gordian II .. A.D. 238

Maximinus I, Balbinus and Pupienus .....A.D. 238

Balbinus and Pupienus .......................A.D. 238

Gordian III .... A.D. 238-244

Philip I ....A.D. 244-247

Philip I and Philip II .... A.D. 247-248

Philip I, Philip II, Pacatian (usurper in Moesia)

      and Jotapian (usurper in

         Syria and Cappadocia) A.D. 248

Philip I and Philip II .... A.D. 248-249

Philip I, Philip II and Trajan Decius ...... A.D. 249

Trajan Decius ................................A.D. 249-251

Trajan Decius and Herennius Etruscus ... A.D. 251

Trebonianus Gallus .... A.D. 251

Trebonianus Gallus and Hostilian .... A.D. 251

Trebonianus Gallus and Volusian ... A.D. 251-253

Trebonianus Gallus, Volusian

        and Aemilian A.D. 253

Aemilian .... A.D. 253

[Uranius Antoninus, usurper in Syria A.D. 253-254]

Aemilian and Valerian .... A.D. 253

Valerian .... A.D. 253

Valerian and Gallienus .... A.D. 253-259

Valerian, Gallienus, Postumus

      (usurper in Gaul) and Saloninus A.D. 259

Valerian, Gallienus and Postumus .... A.D. 259-260

Gallienus, Postumus, Macrianus and

      Quietus (usurpers in the East) A.D. 260-261

[Regalianus, usurper in Pannonia .... A.D. 260]

Gallienus and Postumus ...................A.D. 261-268

Claudius II, Postumus and Laelianus

      (another usurper in Gaul) A.D. 268

[Domitianus, usurper in Gaul ....?A.D. 268]

Claudius II and Marius

      (usurper in Gaul) A.D. 268-269

Claudius II and Victorinus

      (usurper in Gaul) A.D. 269-270

Quintillus and Victorinus .... A.D. 270

Quintillus, Aurelian and Victorinus .... A.D. 270

Aurelian and Victorinus .... A.D. 270

Aurelian and Tetricus

      (usurper in Gaul) A.D. 270-271

Aurelian, Tetricus, Zenobia and Vabalathus

      (usurpers in the East) A.D. 271-272

Aurelian and Tetricus .... A.D. 272-273

Aurelian .... A.D. 273-275

Interregnum (government carried on in the name

      of the widowed empress Severina) A.D. 275

Tacitus .....................................A.D. 275-276

Florian .... A.D. 276

Florian and Probus .... A.D. 276

Probus ......................................A.D. 276-280

Probus and Saturninus

        (usurper in Egypt) A.D. 280

Probus ....A.D. 280-282

Probus and Carus .... A.D. 282

Carus .... A.D. 282-283

Carinus .... A.D. 283

Carinus and Numerian .... A.D. 283-284

Carinus, Diocletian and Julian

        (usurper in Pannonia) A.D. 284-285

Carinus and Diocletian .......................A.D. 285

Diocletian ...................................A.D. 285-286

Diocletian and Maximianus .... A.D. 286-287

Diocletian, Maximianus and Carausius

        (usurper in Britain) A.D. 287-293

Diocletian, Maximianus and Allectus

        (usurper in Britain) A.D. 293-296

Diocletian, Maximianus and Domitius Domitianus

        (usurper in Egypt) A.D. 296-297

Diocletian and Maximianus .... A.D. 297-305

Constantius I and Galerius .... A.D. 305-306

Galerius and Severus II .... A.D. 306

Galerius, Severus II, Maximentius and

      Maximianus (again) A.D. 306-307

Galerius, Maxentius, Maximianus

      and Constantine I A.D. 307-308

Galerius, Licinius, Constantine I

      and Maxentius A.D. 308-309

Galerius, Maximinus II, Licinius,

      Constantine I and Maxentius A.D. 309-310

Galerius, Maximinus II, Licinius, Constantine I,

      Maxentius and Maximianus (again) A.D. 310

Galerius, Maximinus II, Licinius,

      Constantine I and Maxentius A.D. 310-311

Maximinus II, Licinius, Constantine I, Maxentius,

      and Alexander (usurper in N. Africa) A.D. 311

Maximinus II, Licinius, Constantine I

      and Maxentius A.D. 311-312

Maximinus II, Licinius and

      Constantine I A.D. 312-313

Constantine I and Licinius ...............A.D. 313-314

Constantine I, Licinius and Valens .... A.D. 314

Constantine I and Licinius ...............A.D. 314-324

Constantine I, Licinius and Martinian ..... A.D. 324

Constantine I .... A.D. 324-337

Interregnum (government carried on in the

      dead emperor's name) A.D. 337

Constantine II, Constantius II

      and Constans A.D. 337-340

Constantius II and Constans .... A.D. 340-350

Constantius II and Magnentius

      (usurper in the West) A.D. 350

Constantius II, Magnentius and Nepotian

      (usurper at Rome) A.D. 350

Constantius II, Magnentius and Vetranio A.D. 350

Constantius II and Magnentius .... A.D. 350-353

Constantius II .... A.D. 353-360

Constantius II and Julian II .... A.D. 360-361

Julian II .... A.D. 361-363

Jovian .... A.D. 363-364

Valentinian I .... A.D. 364

Valentinian I and Valens .... A.D. 364-365

Valentinian I, Valens and Procopius

      (usurper at Constantinople) A.D. 365-366

Valentinian I and Valens .... A.D. 366-367

Valentinian I, Valens and Gratian .... A.D. 367-375

Valens, Gratian and Valentinian II ... A.D. 375-378

Gratian and Valentinian II ...............A.D. 378-379

Gratian, Theodosius I and

      Valentinian II A.D. 379-383

Gratian, Theodosius I, Valentinian II

      and Arcadius A.D. 383

Gratian, Theodosius I, Valentinian II, Arcadius

      and Magnus Maximus

      (usurper in the West) A.D. 383

Theodosius I, Valentinian II, Arcadius

      and Magnus Maximus A.D. 383-387

Theodosius I, Valentinian II, Arcadius, Magnus

      Maximus and Flavius Victor A.D. 387-388

Theodosius I, Valentinian II
        and Arcadius A.D. 388-392
Theodosius I and Arcadius .... A.D. 392
Theodosius I, Arcadius and Eugenius
        (usurper in the West) A.D. 392-393
Theodosius I, Arcadius, Honorius
        and Eugenius A.D. 393-394
Theodosius I, Arcadius and Honorius A.D. 394-395
Arcadius and Honorius .... A.D. 395-402
Arcadius, Honorius and
        Theodosius II A.D. 402-407
Arcadius, Honorius, Theodosius II
   and Constantine III
        (usurper in the West) A.D. 407-408
Honorius, Theodosius II
        and Constantine III A.D. 408
Honorius, Theodosius II, Constantine III
        and Constans A.D. 408-409
Honorius, Theodosius II, Constantine III,
Constans and Maximus (usurper in Spain) A.D. 409
Honorius, Theodosius II, Constantine III,
   Constans, Maximus and Priscus Attalus
        (usurper at Rome) A.D. 409-410
Honorius, Theodosius II, Constantine III,
   Constans and Maximus A.D. 410-411
Honorius, Theodosius II, Constantine III
        and Maximus A.D. 411
Honorius, Theodosius II
        and Constantine III A.D. 411
Honorius, Theodosius II, Constantine III and
        Jovinus (usurper in Gaul) A.D. 411
Honorius, Theodosius II and Jovinus A.D. 411-412
Honorius, Theodosius II, Jovinus
        and Sebastianus A.D. 412-413
Honorius and Theodosius II .... A.D. 413-414
Honorius, Theodosius II and Priscus Attalus
  (again; usurper in Gaul and Spain) A.D. 414-415
Honorius and Theodosius II .... A.D. 415-421
Honorius, Theodosius II
        and Constantius III A.D. 421

Honorius and Theodosius II .... A.D. 421-423
Theodosius II and Johannes .... A.D. 423-425
Theodosius II and Valentinian III .... A.D. 425-450
Valentinian III and Marcian .............A.D. 450-455
Marcian and Petronius Maximus .... A.D. 455
Marcian (*interregnum* in the West) .... A.D. 455
Marcian and Avitus ...........................A.D. 455-456
Marcian (*interregnum* in the West) ....A.D. 456-457
Leo I (*interregnum* in the West) ..............A.D. 457
Leo I and Majorian .... A.D. 457-461
Leo I (*interregnum* in the West) .... A.D. 461
Leo I and Severus III ........................A.D. 461-465
Leo I (*interregnum* in the West) .... A.D. 465-467
Leo I and Anthemius .... A.D. 467-472
Leo I, Anthemius and Olybrius .... A.D. 472
Leo I and Olybrius .... A.D. 472
Leo I (*interregnum* in the West) .... A.D. 472-473
Leo I and Glycerius ................................A.D. 473
Leo I, Leo II and Glycerius .... A.D. 473-474
Leo II and Glycerius ................................A.D. 474
Leo II, Zeno and Glycerius .......................A.D. 474
Zeno, Leo II and Julius Nepos .... A.D. 474
Zeno and Julius Nepos ......................A.D. 474-475
Basiliscus and Julius Nepos
        (Zeno in exile) A.D. 475
Basiliscus (*interregnum* in the West; Zeno and
        Julius Nepos both in exile) A.D. 475
Basiliscus and Romulus Augustus (Zeno and
     Julius Nepos both in exile) A.D. 475-476
Basiliscus, Marcus and Romulus Augustus (Zeno
        and Julius Nepos both in exile) A.D. 476
Zeno and Romulus Augustus
        (Julius Nepos in exile) A.D. 476
Zeno (the line of Western Emperors ends;
        Julius Nepos in exile) A.D. 476-480
Zeno .... A.D. 480-484
Zeno and Leontius
        (usurper in Asia Minor) A.D. 484-488
Zeno .... A.D. 488-491

PART II

THE BYZANTINE EMPIRE

INTRODUCTION
TO PART II

The accession of Anastasius to the imperial throne of Constantinople (A.D. 491) did not in itself mark an important juncture in the history of the later Roman Empire. Numismatists from the time of Warwick Wroth, in the early part of this century, have adopted the reign of Anastasius I as the most satisfactory starting-point for the Byzantine coinage, and there can be few arguments against this arrangement. Accordingly, I have commenced this listing of Byzantine sovereigns at the year 491, though in a purely historical context Byzantine history could be considered to have begun with the dedication of Constantine's new capital in May, 330.

The most important development of the imperial system in Byzantine times was the firm establishment of the dynastic principle of succession. This concept had never really taken firm root in the earlier days of the Empire and although the first of the great Byzantine imperial dynasties was not founded until 610, there were few emperors after this date who did not belong to a royal house. Indeed, Byzantine sovereignty became so clannish that for the last four centuries of the Empire's existence virtually all the rulers were related to one another. The last emperor, the valiant Constantine XI Palaeologus (1448-53) was the great-great-great-great-great-great-great-great-great-great-grandson of Alexius I who ascended the imperial throne in 1081.

The territorial extent of the realm over which these emperors ruled varied enormously during the millennium of Byzantium's existence. The empire of Anastasius I was the eastern division of the Roman Empire, the western provinces of Britain, Spain, Gaul, Italy and North Africa having succumbed to barbarian invasion. Later in the sixth century Justinian envisaged the reconquest of a large part of the old western division of the Empire, and succeeded in bringing North Africa, Italy and part of Spain back under the control of the imperial government. But this great effort on the part of one idealistic ruler was against the tide of history and in the following century the Empire suffered great territorial losses. These occurred not only in the recently re-conquered western lands but also in the east, where the ancient provinces of Syria, Palestine and Egypt were lost in the first great expansion of Moslem power.

The Heraclian Dynasty (610-711) sowed the seeds of future greatness by carefully re-organizing what was left of the Empire. Their work was built on by later rulers, through centuries of trials and tribulations, until, by the latter part of the tenth century, the Byzantines were able to embark once more on a policy of expansion. Antioch and part of Syria were recovered and the great Basil II, the last effective ruler of the illustrious Macedonian Dynasty, conquered Bulgaria which had for centuries been the Empire's most troublesome neighbour.

The eleventh century was a time of rapid decline and powerful new enemies arose who threatened the very existence of the Christian Empire. The Seljuk Turks overran much of Asia Minor, the very heartland of Byzantine civilization, and at the same time in the west the Normans were threatening what was left of the imperial possessions in Italy. The situation was saved by the genius of Alexius I Comnenus (1081-1118) and the brilliance of the dynasty which he founded staved off the disintegration of the Empire for more than a century.

In 1204 Constantinople was captured by the Christian forces of the Fourth Crusade and remained in Latin hands until the Byzantines recovered their capital fifty-seven years later. During this time Greek resistance was centred on the city of Nicaea in Asia Minor and under the Dynasty of the Lascarids the "empire in exile" flourished and quickly expanded its territory. After the recovery of Constantinople the Empire was ruled by the emperors of the Palaeologan Dynasty right up to the time of its final collapse in 1453. These last two centuries of Byzantine history present a sorrowful picture of an anachronistic state, bent on self-destruction through endless civil wars and continuously threatened by the growing power of the Ottoman Turks. At the end the "Empire" consisted of nothing more than the city of Constantinople itself and the little Despotate of the Morea in southern Greece. The city finally fell to Muhammed the Conqueror on 29th May 1453 thus ending a continuous line of monarchy stretching back to the first Augustus one thousand, four hundred and eighty years before.

Comparing the statistics of the Byzantine emperors with their Roman counterparts one finds that the average Byzantine ruler reigned for almost twice as long — 11¾ years as opposed to 6¼ years. He also survived into his fifty-sixth year, eight years longer than the average Roman emperor. The proportion of Byzantine emperors who died of natural causes in possession of their thrones (45%) is very high in relation to the Roman Empire (31%). This can be explained by the firm establishment of the dynastic principle at Constantinople. Loyalty to a popular dynasty often ensured the survival of a second-rate ruler who, under different circumstances, would almost certainly have been removed to make way for a stronger rival.

The ten longest reigns in Byzantine history are:

1. Basil II, reigned for 49 years, 11 months, 5 days.
2. John V, reigned for 49 years, 8 months, 1 day.
3. Constantine VII, reigned for 46 years, 5 months, 3 days.
4. Andronicus II, reigned for 45 years, 5 months, 13 days.
5. Justinian I, reigned for 38 years, 3 months, 13 days.
6. Manuel I, reigned for 37 years, 5 months, 16 days.
7. Alexius I, reigned for 37 years, 4 months, 11 days.
8. Constantine V, reigned for 34 years, 2 months, 27 days.
9. Manuel II, reigned for 32 years (approx.)
10. John III, reigned for 32 years (approx.)

INDEX :   A. REIGNING EMPERORS AND EMPRESSES

In the following lists an asterisk indicates that the emperor, empress or co-emperor is not known to have issued coins (or to have had them struck in their honour).

B. EMPRESSES AND PRINCESSES

(Other than those who reigned in their own right).

Thecla, d. of THEOPHILUS (163), s. of MICHAEL III (164).
*Theodora, w. of JUSTINIAN I (135).
*Theodora, w. of JUSTINIAN II (148).
Theodora, w. of THEOPHILUS (163), m. of MICHAEL III (164).
*Theodora, s. of ROMANUS II (170), w. of JOHN I (172).
*Theodora, d. of ALEXIUS I (191), grandm. of ISAAC II (197) and ALEXIUS III (198).
*Theodora, w. of MICHAEL VIII (205).
*Theodora, d. of JOHN VI (209).
*Theophano, w. of LEO VI (166).
*Theophano, w. of ROMANUS II (170) and of NICEPHORUS II (171).

*Xene (Maria) of Armenia, w. of Michael IX (co-emperor 1295-1320), m. of ANDRONICUS III (207).

Zoe Carbonopsina, w. of LEO VI (166), m. of CONSTANTINE VII (168).
Zoe Zautzina, w. of LEO VI (166).

Andronicus, s. of CONSTANTINE X (183) and EUDOCIA (184,186), *co-emperor* 1068-71 with
      ROMANUS IV (185).
*Bardas Caesar, uncle of MICHAEL III (164), † 865.

Christopher, *co-emperor* 921-31 with his father ROMANUS I (169) and brother-in-law
      CONSTANTINE VII (168).
Constantine, *co-emperor* 813-20 with his father LEO V (161).
Constantine, *co-emperor* 830-*circa* 835 with his father THEOPHILUS (163).
Constantine, *co-emperor* 868-77 with his father BASIL I (165).
Constantine, *co-emperor* 924-45 with his father ROMANUS I (169) and brother-in-law CONSTANTINE
      VII (168).
Constantine, s. of CONSTANTINE X (183), *co-emperor* in 1067 with his mother EUDOCIA (184,186)
      and from 1068-1071 with ROMANUS IV (185).
*Constantine, s. of MICHAEL VII (187) and Maria.
*Constantine Angelus, s.-in-law of ALEXIUS I (191), grandf. of ISAAC II (197) and ALEXIUS III (198).

Heraclius, exarch of Carthage, f. of HERACLIUS (140).
Heraclius, *co-emperor* 659-668 with his father CONSTANS II (143) and 668-681 with his brother
      CONSTANTINE IV (144).

*Isaac, s. of ALEXIUS I (191), f. of ANDRONICUS I (195).

*John Ducas Caesar, uncle of MICHAEL VII (187), grandf. of Irene Dukaina.

*Manuel, s. of JOHN VI (209), despot of the Morea.
*Matthew, *co-emperor* in 1354 with his father JOHN VI (209).
Michael (IX), *co-emperor* 1295-1320 with his father ANDRONICUS II (206).

Nicephorus, *co-emperor* 742-3 with his father ARTAVASDUS (153).
*Nicetas, s. of ARTAVASDUS (153).

Stephen, *co-emperor* 924-45 with his father ROMANUS I (169) and brother-in-law CONSTANTINE
      VII (168).

Theodosius, *co-emperor circa* 589-602 with his father MAURICE TIBERIUS (138).
Theophylactus, *co-emperor* 811-13 with his father MICHAEL I (160).
Tiberius, *co-emperor* 659-668 with his father CONSTANS II (143) and 668-681 with his brother
      CONSTANTINE IV (144).
Tiberius, *co-emperor* 705-11 with his father JUSTINIAN II (148).

THE AGE OF JUSTINIAN

Emperor	Born	Succeeded	Relationship to Predecessors	Died	Cause of Death, Age	Length of Reign	Relatives	Contemporary Rulers
133. ANASTASIUS I	Circa 430 at Dyrrachium.	11 April, 491, having been selected by Ariadne, widow of Zeno.	None.	1 July, 518.	Natural causes, aged approx. 88.	27 years, 2 months, 20 days.	Wife: Aelia Ariadne (d. of Leo I), m. 491, d. 515.	Sassanian Empire: Kavadh I (first reign 488-96); Jamasp (496-98/9); Kavadh I (second reign 498/9-531). Ostrogoths in Italy: Theodoric (493-526). Vandals in N. Africa: Gunthamund (484-96); Trasamund (496-523).
134. JUSTIN I	450 or 452, at Bederiana, (near Skopje).	10 July, 518.	None.	1 Aug., 527.	Natural causes, aged 77 or 75.	9 years, 22 days.	Nephew: Justinian I, EMPEROR 527-65.	Sassanian Empire: Kavadh I (second reign 498/9-531). Ostrogoths in Italy: Theodoric (493-526); Athalaric (526-34). Vandals in N. Africa: Trasamund (496-523); Hilderic (523-30).
135. JUSTINIAN I (originally named Petrus Sabbatius)	483, at Taurisium (near Skopje)	Made co-emperor by Justin I, 4 April, 527; sole emperor from 1 Aug., 527.	Nephew of Justin I.	14 Nov., 565.	Natural causes, aged 82.	38 years, 3 months, 13 days.	Wife: Theodora, m. 523, d. 548. Nephew: Justin II, EMPEROR 565-78.	Sassanian Empire: Kavadh I (second reign 498/9-531); Khosrau I (531-79). Ostrogoths in Italy: Athalaric (526-34); Theodahad (534-6); Witigis (536-40); Ildibad (540-41); Eraric (541); Baduila = Totila (541-52); Theia (552-3). Vandals in N. Africa: Hilderic (523-30); Gelimer (530-33).
136. JUSTIN II	Date of birth unknown.	15 Nov., 565.	Nephew of Justinian I.	5 Oct., 578.	Natural causes, age unknown.	12 years, 10 months, 20 days.	Wife: Sophia (niece of Theodora).	Sassanian Empire: Khosrau I (531-79).
137. TIBERIUS II CONSTANTINE	Date of birth unknown; of Thracian origin.	Appointed Caesar, Dec., 574, and made co-emperor with Justin II 26 Sept., 578; sole emperor from 5 Oct., 578.	None.	14 Aug., 582.	Natural causes, age unknown.	3 years, 10 months, 9 days. [7 years and 8 months from his appointment as Caesar.]	Wife: Anastasia. Daughter: Constantina.	Sassanian Empire: Khosrau I (531-79); Ormizd IV (579-90).
138. MAURICE TIBERIUS	Circa 539, in Cappadocia.	Crowned by Tiberius II 13 Aug., 582 and became sole emperor the following day.	None.	25 Nov., 602.	Executed following his flight to Asia Minor after the successful rebellion of Phocas. Age approx. 63.	20 years, 3 months, 8 days (up to his deposition on 22 Nov., 602).	Wife: Constantina (d. of Tiberius II), m. 582. Son: Theodosius, CO-EMPEROR circa 589-602.	Sassanian Empire: Ormizd IV (579-90); Khosrau II (first reign 590); Bahram VI (590-91); Khosrau II (second reign 591-628).
139. PHOCAS	Date of birth unknown; of Thracian origin.	23 Nov., 602, following the deposition of Maurice Tiberius.	None.	5 Oct., 610.	Executed following the successful rebellion of Heraclius. Age unknown.	7 years, 10 months, 12 days.	Wife: Leontia.	Sassanian Empire: Khosrau II (second reign 591-628).

THE HERACLIAN DYNASTY

Emperor	Born	Succeeded	Relationship to Predecessors	Died	Cause of Death, Age	Length of Reign	Relatives	Contemporary Rulers
140. HERACLIUS	Circa 575, in Cappadocia.	Rebelled against Phocas, summer 608. Eventually crowned in Constantinople, 5 Oct., 610.	None.	11 Jan., 641	Natural causes, aged approx. 66.	30 years, 3 months, 6 days.	Father: Heraclius, exarch of Carthage at the time of the rebellion against Phocas. Wife: 1. Fabia-Eudocia, d. 612. 2. Martina (his niece), m. 614. Sons: Heraclius Constantine (by Fabia-Eudocia), EMPEROR 641. Heraclonas (by Martina), EMPEROR 641. Grandson: Constans II, EMPEROR 641-68.	Sassanian Empire: Khosrau II (second reign 591-628); Kavadh II (628); Ardashir III (628-30); Shahrvaraz (630); Borandukht (630-31); Ormizd V (631-2); Yazdegerd III (632-51). Arab Caliphate: Abu Bekr (632-4); Omar I (634-44).
141. HERACLIUS CONSTANTINE	3 May, 612.	11 Jan., 641 [but had been co-emperor with Heraclius from 22 Jan., 613].	Son of Heraclius.	20 April, 641.	Probably natural causes, aged 29.	3 months, 9 days.	Mother: Fabia-Eudocia, d. 612. Son: Constans II, EMPEROR 641-68. Half-brother: Heraclonas, EMPEROR 641.	Sassanian Empire: Yazdegerd III (632-51). Arab Caliphate: Omar I (634-44).
142. HERACLONAS	625/6.	20 April, 641 [but had been co-emperor with Heraclius and Heraclius Constantine from 4 July, 638].	Half-brother of Heraclius Constantine; Son of Heraclius.	Deposed and exiled October 641. Date of death unknown.	Unknown.	Approx. 6 months.	Mother: Martina, exiled with her son, October 641.	(Same as last).
143. CONSTANS II (Officially named Constantine, but popularly abbreviated to Constans).	7 Nov., 630.	Crowned co-emperor by Heraclonas, September 641 and became sole emperor the following month when Heraclonas was deposed.	Nephew of Heraclonas. Son of Heraclius Constantine; Grandson of Heraclius.	15 July, 668, at Syracuse.	Assassinated. Age 38.	26 years, 9 months (approx.)	Sons: Constantine IV, EMPEROR 668-85. Heraclius, CO-EMPEROR 2 June, 659 till autumn 681. Tiberius, CO-EMPEROR 2 June, 659 till autumn 681.	Sassanian Empire: Yazdegerd III (632-51). Arab Caliphate: Omar I (634-44); Othman (644-56); Ali (656-61); Muawija I (661-80, first of the Umayyads).
144. CONSTANTINE IV	Circa 652.	15 July, 668, though not proclaimed at Constantinople before September. [Had been co-emperor with Constans II from 13 April, 654].	Son of Constans II; Grandson of Heraclius Constantine; Great-grandson of Heraclius.	10 July, 685.	Natural causes, aged approx. 33.	17 years, all but 5 days. [31 years, 2 months, 27 days from his elevation to the rank of co-emperor].	Son: Justinian II, EMPEROR 685-95 and 705-11. Brothers: Heraclius, CO-EMPEROR up to the autumn of 681. Tiberius, CO-EMPEROR up to the autumn of 681.	Umayyad Caliphs: Muawija I (661-80); Jezid I (680-83); Muawija II (683-4); Merwan I (684-5); Abdalmalik (685-705). Bulgaria: Asparuch (680-701).

Emperor	Born	Succeeded	Relationship to Predecessors	Died	Cause of Death, Age	Length of Reign	Relatives	Contemporary Rulers
145. JUSTINIAN II (first reign)	669.	10 July, 685.	Son of Constantine IV; Grandson of Constans II; Great-grandson of Heraclius Constantine; Great-great-grandson of Heraclius.	*Deposed* and exiled late in 695.		Approx. 10¼ years.		**Umayyad Caliphs:** Abdalmalik (685-705). **Bulgaria:** Asparuch (680-701).
		First Reign				Second Reign		
146. LEONTIUS	Date of birth unknown.	Rebelled against Justinian II late in 695.	None.	*Deposed* late in 698. Ultimately executed by Justinian II in 705.	Age unknown.	Approx. 3 years.		(Same as last).
147. TIBERIUS III (Apsimar).	Date of birth unknown.	Rebelled against Leontius late in 698.	None.	*Deposed* in the summer of 705 and later executed with Leontius by Justinian II.	Age unknown.	Approx. 6½ years.		**Umayyad Caliphs:** Abdalmalik (685-705). **Bulgaria:** Asparuch (680-701); Tervel (701-18).
148. JUSTINIAN II (second reign)	669.	Overthrew Tiberius III, summer 705.	[See under first reign, no. 145].	4 Nov., 711.	Executed following the successful rebellion of Philippicus. Age 42.	Approx. 6¼ years.	*Wife:* Theodora (sister of the Khazar Khan). *Son:* Tiberius, CO-EMPEROR 705-11.	**Umayyad Caliphs:** Abdalmalik (685-705); Walid I (705-15). **Bulgaria:** Tervel (701-18).
149. PHILIPPICUS (Bardanes).	Date of birth unknown.	Rebelled against Justinian II and became emperor, 4 Nov., 711.	None.	*Deposed* 3 June, 713. Date of death unknown.	Unknown.	1 year, 7 months (all but one day).		**Umayyad Caliphs:** Walid I (705-15). **Bulgaria:** Tervel (701-18).
150. ANASTASIUS II (Artemius).	Date of birth unknown.	3 June, 713, following the deposition of Philippicus.	None.	*Deposed* summer 715. Ultimately executed by Leo III following an unsuccessful revolt, 721.	Age unknown.	Probably a little over 2 years.		(Same as last).
151. THEODOSIUS III of Adramytium.	Date of birth unknown.	Summer, 715, following the deposition of Anastasius II.	None.	*Deposed* 24 July, 717. Date of death unknown.	Unknown.	Approx. 2 years.		**Umayyad Caliphs:** Suleiman (715-17) and Omar II (715-20). **Bulgaria:** Tervel (701-18).

Emperor	Born	Succeeded	Relationship to Predecessors	Died	Cause of Death, Age	Length of Reign	Relatives	Contemporary Rulers
152. LEO III the 'Isaurian.	Circa 680, at Germanicia in Commagene.	Proclaimed emperor by his troops 25 March, 717 in opposition to Theodosius III who was later overthrown.	None.	18 June, 741.	Natural causes, aged approx. 61.	24 years, 2 months. 24 days.	Son: Constantine V, EMPEROR 741-75. Son-in-law: Artavasdus, EMPEROR 742-3.	Umayyad Caliphs: Omar II (715-20); Jezid II (720-24); Hischam (724-43). Bulgaria: Tervel (701-18); unknown Khan (718-24); Sevar (724-39); Kormisos (739-56).
153. ARTAVASDUS	Date of birth unknown.	Proclaimed emperor by his troops July 742 in opposition to Constantine V who fled to Amorium.	Son-in-law of Leo III; Brother-in-law of Constantine V.	Deposed 2 Nov., 743. Date of death unknown.	Unknown.	1 year, 4 months. (approx.)	Wife: Anna (d. of Leo III and sis. of Constantine V). Sons: Nicephorus, CO-EMPEROR. Nicetas.	Umayyad Caliphs: Hischam (724-43). Walid II (743-4). Bulgaria: Kormisos (739-56).
154. CONSTANTINE V, Copronymus.	718.	18 June, 741. [Had been co-emperor with Leo III from 25 March, 720].	Son of Leo III.	14 Sept., 775.	Natural causes, aged 57.	34 years, 2 months, 27 days.	Son: Leo IV, EMPEROR 775-80. Grandson: Constantine VI, EMPEROR 780-97. Brother-in-law: Artavasdus, EMPEROR 742-3.	Umayyad Caliphs: Hischam (724-43); Walid II (743-4); Jezid III (744); Ibrahim (744); Merwan II (744-50). Abbasid Caliphs: as-Saffach (750-54); al-Mansur (754-75). Bulgaria: Kormisos (739-56); Vinech (756-62); Teletz (762-4); Sabin (764-6); Umar, Toktu (766); Pagan (767-70); Telerig (770-77). Carolingians: Pepin III, the Short (751-68); Charlemagne (768-814). Popes (from 752): Stephen II (752-7); Paul I (757-67); Stephen III (768-72); Adrian I (772-95).
155. LEO IV the Khazar.	749.	14 Sept., 775. [Had been co-emperor with Constantine V from 751].	Son of Constantine V; Grandson of Leo III.	8 Sept., 780.	Natural causes, aged 31.	5 years (all but 6 days).	Wife: Irene, EMPRESS 797-802. Son: Constantine VI, EMPEROR 780-97.	Abbasid Caliphs: al-Machdi (775-85). Bulgaria: Telerig (770-77); Kardam (777-803). Carolingians: Charlemagne (768-814). Popes: Adrian I (772-95).
156. CONSTANTINE VI	770.	8 Sept., 780. [Had been co-emperor with Leo IV from 24 April, 776].	Son of Leo IV; Grandson of Constantine V; Great-grandson of Leo III.	Deposed 19 Aug., 797. Date of death unknown.	Unknown.	16 years, 11 months, 11 days.	Mother: Irene, EMPRESS 797-802, and CO-RULER throughout most of her son's reign.	Abbasid Caliphs: al-Machdi (775-85); al-Hadi (785-6); Harun al-Raschid (786-809). Bulgaria: Kardam (777-803). Carolingians: Charlemagne (768-814). Popes: Adrian I (772-95); Leo III (795-816).
157. IRENE (Empress).	Circa 752 in Athens.	19 Aug., 797. [Had been co-ruler with her son Constantine VI throughout most of his reign].	Mother of Constantine VI; Widow of Leo IV; Daughter-in-law of Constantine V.	Deposed 31 Oct., 802 and exiled to Lesbos where she died the following year.	Probably natural causes, aged approx. 51.	5 years, 2 months, 12 days.		Abbasid Caliphs: Harun al-Raschid (786-809). Bulgaria: Kardam (777-803). Carolingians: Charlemagne (768-814; crowned 'Roman Emperor' by Pope Leo III in 800). Popes: Leo III (795-816).
158. NICEPHORUS I	In Seleucia (Pisidia). Date unknown.	1 Nov., 802, following the deposition of Irene.	None.	25 July, 811, in the Bulgarian mountains.	Killed in battle against the Bulgar Khan Krum. Age unknown.	8 years, 8 months, 24 days.	Son: Stauracius, EMPEROR 811.	Abbasid Caliphs: Harun al-Raschid (786-809); al-Amin (809-13). Bulgaria: Kardam (777-803); Krum (803-14). Carolingians: Charlemagne (768-814). Popes: Leo III (795-816).

Emperor	Born	Succeeded	Relationship to Predecessors	Died	Cause of Death, Age	Length of Reign	Relatives	Contemporary Rulers
159. STAURACIUS	Date of birth unknown.	25 July, 811. [Had been co-emperor with Nicephorus I from December 803].	Son of Nicephorus I.	*Abdicated* 2 Oct., 811 in favour of Michael Rhangabe. Died about 3 months later.	Wounds sustained in the battle against Krum. Age unknown.	2 months, 7 days.	*Brother-in-law:* Michael I, EMPEROR 811-13.	**Abbasid Caliphs:** al-Amin (809-13). **Bulgaria:** Krum (803-14). **Carolingians:** Charlemagne (768-814). **Popes:** Leo III (795-816).
160. MICHAEL I Rhangabe.	Date of birth unknown.	2 Oct., 811 on the abdication of Stauracius.	Brother-in-law of Stauracius; Son-in-law of Nicephorus I.	*Deposed* 11 July, 813. Date of death unknown.	Unknown.	1 year, 9 months, 9 days.	*Son:* Theophylactus, CO-EMPEROR from 25 Dec. 811	(Same as last).
161. LEO V the Armenian.	Date of birth unknown.	11 July, 813, following the deposition of Michael I.	None.	25 Dec., 820.	Assassinated before the high altar of Hagia Sophia. Age unknown.	7 years, 5 months, 14 days.	*Son:* Constantine, CO-EMPEROR from 25 Dec., 813.	**Abbasid Caliphs:** al-Mamun (813-33). **Bulgaria:** Krum (803-14); Dukum, Dicevg (814); Omurtag (814-31). **Carolingians:** Charlemagne (768-814); Louis I, the Pious (first reign 814-33). **Popes:** Leo III (795-816); Stephen IV (816-17); Paschal I (817-24).
162. MICHAEL II the Amorian.	In Amorium (Phrygia), date unknown.	25 Dec., 820, following the assassination of Leo V.	None.	2 Oct., 829.	Natural causes, age unknown.	8 years, 9 months, 7 days.	*Son:* Theophilus, EMPEROR 829-42.	**Abbasid Caliphs:** al-Mamun (813-33). **Bulgaria:** Omurtag (814-31). **Carolingians:** Louis I, the Pious (first reign 814-33). **Popes:** Paschal I (817-24); Eugenius II (824-7); Valentinus (827); Gregory IV (827-44).
163. THEOPHILUS	Date of birth unknown.	2 Oct., 829. [Had been co-emperor with Michael II from 12 May, 821].	Son of Michael II.	20 Jan., 842.	Natural causes, age unknown.	12 years, 3 months, 18 days.	*Wife:* Theodora. *Sons:* Constantine, CO-EMPEROR 5 June, 830-*circa* 835. Michael III, EMPEROR 842-67. *Daughters:* Thecla, Anna and Anastasia.	**Abbasid Caliphs:** al-Mamun (813-33); al-Mutasim (833-42). **Bulgaria:** Omurtag (814-31); Malomir/Presiam (831-52). **Carolingians:** Louis I, the Pious (first reign 814-33); Lothair I (833-4); Louis I (second reign 834-40). **Popes:** Gregory IV (827-44).
164. MICHAEL III 'the Drunkard'.	*Circa* 836.	20 Jan., 842. [Had been co-emperor with Theophilus from 1 Sept., 840].	Son of Theophilus; Grandson of Michael II.	23 Sept., 867.	Murdered by his co-emperor Basil I. Age approx. 31.	25 years, 8 months, 3 days.	*Mother:* Theodora. [*Mistress:* Eudocia Ingerina, later wife of Basil I]. *Sister:* Thecla. *Uncle:* Bardas Caesar, assassinated 865.	**Abbasid Caliphs:** al-Wathik (842-7); al-Mutawakkil (847-61); al-Muntasir (861-2); al-Mutazz (862-6); al-Muchtadi (866-9). **Bulgaria:** Malomir/Presiam (831-52); Boris I Michael (852-89). **Popes:** Gregory IV (827-44); Sergius II (844-7); Leo IV (847-55); Benedict III (855-8); Nicholas I (858-67).

THE MACEDONIAN DYNASTY

Emperor	Born	Succeeded	Relationship to Predecessors	Died	Cause of Death, Age	Length of Reign	Relatives	Contemporary Rulers
165. BASIL I the Macedonian.	Date of birth unknown.	23 Sept., 867. [Had been co-emperor with Michael III from 26 May, 866]	None.	28 Aug., 886.	Natural causes, age unknown.	18 years, 11 months, 5 days.	*Wife*: 1. Maria. 2. Eudocia Ingerina, formerly mistress of Michael III *Sons*: Constantine (by Maria), CO-EMPEROR 10 Feb., 868- 3 Sept., 877. Leo VI (by Eudocia), EMPEROR 886-912. Alexander (by Eudocia), EMPEROR 912-13.	**Abbasid Caliphs**: al-Muchtadi (866-9); al-Mutamid (869-92). **Bulgaria**: Boris I Michael (852-89). **Popes**: Adrian II (867-72); John VIII (872-82); Marinus I (882-4); Adrian III (884-5); Stephen V (885-91).
166. LEO VI the Wise.	Sept., 866.	28 Aug., 886. [Had been co-emperor with Basil I from 6 Jan., 870].	Son of Basil I	11 May, 912.	Natural causes, aged 46.	25 years, 8 months, 13 days.	*Wife*: 1. Theophano. 2. Zoe Zautzina. 3. Eudocia. 4. Zoe Carbonopsina. *Son*: Constantine VII (by Zoe Carbonopsina), EMPEROR 913-59. *Brother*: Alexander, EMPEROR 912-13.	**Abbasid Caliphs**: al-Mutamid (869-92); al-Mutadid (892-902); al-Muktafi (902-8); al-Muktadir (908-32). **Bulgaria**: Boris I Michael (852-89); Vladimir (889-93); Symeon (893-927). **Popes**: Stephen V (885-91); Formosus (891-6); Boniface VI (896); Stephen VI (896-7); Romanus (897); Theodore II (897); John IX (898-900); Benedict IV (900-03); Leo V (903); Sergius III (904-11); Anastasius III (911-13).
167. ALEXANDER	23 Nov., 871.	11 May, 912. [Had been co-emperor with Leo VI throughout his reign, and with Basil I from Sept., 877].	Brother of Leo VI; Son of Basil I.	6 June, 913.	Natural causes, aged 42.	1 year, 26 days.	*Nephew*: Constantine VII, EMPEROR 913-59.	**Abbasid Caliphs**: al-Muktadir (908-32). **Bulgaria**: Symeon (893-927). **Popes**: Anastasius III (911-13).
168. CONSTANTINE VII, Porphyrogenitus.	18 May, 905.	6 June, 913. [Had been co-emperor during Alexander's reign, and with Leo VI from 15 May, 908].	Nephew of Alexander; Son of Leo VI; Grandson of Basil I.	9 Nov., 959.	Natural causes, aged 54.	46 years, 5 months, 3 days.	*Mother*: Zoe Carbonopsina, regent 914-19. *Wife*: Helena (d. of Romanus I). *Son*: Romanus II, EMPEROR 959-63. *Grandsons*: Basil II, EMPEROR 976-1025. Constantine VIII, EMPEROR 1025-8. *Father-in-law*: Romanus I, EMPEROR 920-44. *Brothers-in-law*: Christopher, Stephen and Constantine, CO-EMPERORS (see under Romanus I).	**Abbasid Caliphs**: al-Muktadir (908-32); al-Kahir (932-4); al-Radi (934-40); al-Muttaki (940-43); al-Mustakfi (943-6); al-Muti (946-74). **Bulgaria**: Symeon (893-927); Peter (927-69). **Germany**: Otto I, the Great (936-73). **Popes**: Lando (913-14); John X (914-28); Leo VI (928); Stephen VII (929-31); John XI (931-5); Leo VII (936-9); Stephen VIII (939-42); Marinus II (942-6); Agapetus II (946-55); John XII (955-64).

Emperor	Born	Succeeded	Relationship to Predecessors	Died	Cause of Death, Age	Length of Reign	Relatives	Contemporary Rulers
169. ROMANUS I Lecapenus.	Circa 870.	Proclaimed co-emperor with Constantine VII 17 Dec., 920.	None.	Deposed 16 Dec., 944 and exiled to Prote where he died 15 June, 948.	Natural causes, aged approx. 78.	24 years (all but one day).	Son-in-law: Constantine VII, EMPEROR 913-59. Sons: Christopher, CO-EMPEROR 20 May, 921-August 931; Stephen, CO-EMPEROR 25 Dec., 924-27 Jan., 945. Constantine, CO-EMPEROR 25 Dec., 924- 27 Jan., 945. Daughter: Helena (w. of Constantine VII). Grandson: Romanus II, EMPEROR 959-63.	(See under Constantine VII).
170. ROMANUS II	938.	9 Nov., 959 [Had been co-emperor with Constantine VII from 6 April, 945].	Son of Constantine VII; Grandson of Romanus I and of Leo VI; Great-grandson of Basil I.	15 March, 963.	Probably natural causes, aged 25.	3 years, 4 months, 6 days.	Wife: Theophano. Sons: Basil II, EMPEROR 976-1025; Constantine VIII, EMPEROR 1025-8. Sister: Theodora.	**Abbasid Caliphs:** al-Muti (946-74). **Bulgaria:** Peter (927-69). **Germany:** Otto I, the Great (936-73). **Popes:** John XII (955-64).
171. NICEPHORUS II Phocas.	Circa 912.	16 Aug., 963. (5 months after the death of Romanus II, during which time Theophano had acted as regent for her sons).	None.	10 Dec., 969.	Assassinated. Age approx. 57.	6 years, 3 months, 24 days.	Wife: Theophano (widow of Romanus II). Stepsons: Basil II, EMPEROR 976-1025. Constantine VIII, EMPEROR 1025-8.	**Abbasid Caliphs:** al-Muti (946-74). **Bulgaria:** Peter (927-69); Boris II (969-72). **Germany:** Otto I, the Great (936-73). **Popes:** John XII (955-64); Leo VIII (963-5); John XIII (965-72).
172. JOHN I Tzimisces.	924.	11 Dec., 969 following his assassination of Nicephorus II.	None.	10 Jan., 976.	Natural causes, aged 52.	6 years, 1 month (all but one day).	Wife: Theodora (sis. of Romanus II). Nephews (by marriage): Basil II, EMPEROR 976-1025; Constantine VIII, EMPEROR 1025-8.	**Abbasid Caliphs:** al-Muti (946-74); at-Tai (974-91). **Bulgaria:** Boris II (969-72). **Germany:** Otto I, the Great (936-73); Otto II (973-83). **Popes:** John XIII (965-72); Benedict VI (973-4); Benedict VII (974-83).
173. BASIL II Bulgaroktonos.	Circa 957.	10 Jan., 976. [Had been co-emperor with Romanus II from April, 960, with Nicephorus II 963-9, and with John I 969-76].	Son of Romanus II; Grandson of Constantine VII; Great-grandson of Leo VI and of Romanus I; Great-great-grandson of Basil I.	15 Dec., 1025.	Natural causes, aged approx. 68.	50 years (all but 26 days).	Brother: Constantine VIII, EMPEROR 1025-8. Sister: Anna (w. of Vladimir of Kiev). Nieces: Eudocia. Zoe, EMPRESS 1042. Theodora, EMPRESS 1042 and 1055-6.	**Abbasid Caliphs:** at-Tai (974-91); al-Kadir (991-1031). **Bulgaria:** Samuel (976-1014); Gabriel Radomir (1014-15); John Vladislav (1015-18). **Germany:** Otto II (973-83); Otto III (983-1002); Henry II (1002-1024); Conrad II (1024-39). **Popes:** Benedict VII (974-83); John XIV (983-4); John XV (985-96); Gregory V (996-9); Silvester II (999-1003); John XVII (1003); John XVIII (1004-9); Sergius IV (1009-12); Benedict VIII (1012-24); John XIX (1024-32).

Emperor	Born	Succeeded	Relationship to Predecessors	Died	Cause of Death, Age	Length of Reign	Relatives	Contemporary Rulers
174. CONSTANTINE VIII	958.	15 Dec., 1025. [Had been co-emperor with Romanus II from April, 961, with Nicephorus II 963-9, with John I 969-76, and with Basil II 976-1025].	Brother of Basil II; Son of Romanus II; Grandson of Constantine VII; Great-grandson of Leo VI and of Romanus I; Great-great-grandson of Basil I.	11 Nov., 1028.	Natural causes, aged 70.	2 years, 10 months, 27 days.	*Daughters*: Eudocia. Zoe, EMPRESS 1042. Theodora, EMPRESS 1042 and 1055-6. *Son-in-law*: Romanus III, EMPEROR 1028-34.	**Abbasid Caliphs**: al-Kadir (991-1031). **Germany**: Conrad II (1024-39). **Popes**: John XIX (1024-32).
175. ROMANUS III Argyrus.	*Circa* 968.	12 Nov., 1028.	Son-in-law of Constantine VIII.	11 April, 1034.	Assassinated. Age approx. 66.	5 years, 5 months (all but one day).	*Wife*: Zoe (d. of Constantine VIII), EMPRESS 1042.	**Abbasid Caliphs**: al-Kadir (991-1031); al-Kaim (1031-75). **Germany**: Conrad II (1024-39). **Popes**: John XIX (1024-32); Benedict IX (1032-45).
176. MICHAEL IV the Paphlagonian.	Date of birth unknown.	12 April, 1034.	None.	10 Dec., 1041.	Natural causes. Age unknown.	7 years, 8 months (all but 2 days).	*Wife*: Zoe (d. of Constantine VIII, widow of Romanus III), EMPRESS 1042. *Nephew*: Michael V, EMPEROR 1041-2.	**Abbasid Caliphs**: al-Kaim (1031-75). **Germany**: Conrad II (1024-39); Henry III (1039-56). **Popes**: Benedict IX (1032-45).
177. MICHAEL V Kalaphates.	Date of birth unknown.	10 Dec., 1041.	Nephew of Michael IV.	*Deposed* 21 April, 1042. Date of death unknown.	Unknown.	4 months, 11 days.		**Abbasid Caliphs**: al-Kaim (1031-75). **Germany**: Henry III (1039-56). **Popes**: Benedict IX (1032-45).
178. ZOE (*Empress*).	*Circa* 978	21 April, 1042 following the deposition of Michael V.	Widow of Michael IV and of Romanus III; Daughter of Constantine VIII; Niece of Basil II; Granddaughter of Romanus II; Great-granddaughter of Constantine VII; Great-great-granddaughter of Leo VI and of Romanus I; Great-great-great-granddaughter of Basil I.	*Abdicated* 12 June 1042 in favour of her third husband, Constantine Monomachus, during whose reign she died.	Natural causes, in her late sixties or early seventies.	7 weeks, 3 days.	*Sisters*: Eudocia. Theodora, CO-EMPRESS throughout the reign, and EMPRESS 1055-6.	(Same as last).
179. CONSTANTINE IX, Monomachus.	*Circa* 980.	12 June, 1042, following his marriage to Zoe and the abdication of Zoe and Theodora.	Husband of Zoe.	11 Jan., 1055.	Natural causes, aged approx. 75.	12 years, 7 months (all but one day).	*Wife*: Zoe (d. of Constantine VIII, widow of Romanus III and Michael IV), EMPRESS 1042. *Sister-in-law*: Theodora, EMPRESS 1042 and 1055-6.	**Abbasid Caliphs**: al-Kaim (1031-75). **Germany**: Henry III (1039-56). **Popes**: Benedict IX (1032-45); Gregory VI (1045-6); Clement II (1046-7); Benedict IX, again (1047-8); Damasus II (1048); Leo IX (1049-54).

Romanus III   Michael IV   Constantine IX

Emperor	Born	Succeeded	Relationship to Predecessors	Died	Cause of Death, Age	Length of Reign	Relatives	Contemporary Rulers
180. THEODORA (*Empress*).	Exact date uncertain, but younger than her sister Zoe.	11 Jan., 1055.	Sister-in-law of Constantine IX, Michael IV and Romanus III; Sister of Zoe; Daughter of Constantine VIII, etc., etc. (see under Zoe).	21 Aug., 1056.	Natural causes. Age unknown.	1 year, 7 months, 10 days.		**Abbasid Caliphs:** al-Kaim (1031-75). **Germany:** Henry III (1039-56). **Popes:** Victor II (1055-7).
181. MICHAEL VI Stratioticus.	Date of birth unknown, but was already elderly at the time of his accession.	21 Aug., 1056.	None.	*Deposed* 31 Aug., 1057. Date of death unknown.	Unknown	1 year and 10 days.		**Abbasid Caliphs:** al-Kaim (1031-75). **Germany:** Henry III (1039-56); Henry IV (1056-1106). **Popes:** Victor II (1055-7); Stephen IX (1057-8).

THE DYNASTIES OF THE DUCAS AND THE COMNENI

Emperor	Born	Succeeded	Relationship to Predecessors	Died	Cause of Death, Age	Length of Reign	Relatives	Contemporary Rulers
182. ISAAC I Comnenus.	Circa 1005.	1 Sept., 1057, following the deposition of Michael VI.	None.	Abdicated 25 Dec., 1059 and retired to the Studite monastery, where he died two years later.	Natural causes, aged approx. 57.	2 years, 3 months, 24 days.	Nephew: Alexius I, EMPEROR 1081-1118.	**Abbasid Caliphs:** al-Kaim (1031-75). **Germany:** Henry IV (1056-1106). **Popes:** Stephen IX (1057-8); Nicholas II (1059-61). **Normans:** Robert Guiscard, duke of Apulia (1059-85).
183. CONSTANTINE X, Ducas.	Circa 1007.	25 Dec., 1059, following the abdication of Isaac I.	None.	21 May, 1067.	Natural causes, aged approx. 60.	7 years, 4 months, 26 days.	Wife: Eudocia Macrembolitissa, EMPRESS 1067 and 1071. Sons: Michael VII, EMPEROR 1071-8; Andronicus; Constantine.	**Abbasid Caliphs:** al-Kaim (1031-75). **Germany:** Henry IV (1056-1106). **Popes:** Nicholas II (1059-61); Alexander II (1061-73). **Normans:** Robert Guiscard, duke of Apulia (1059-85).
184. EUDOCIA (Empress).	Circa 1021.	21 May, 1067.	Widow of Constantine X.	Abdicated 31 Dec., 1067 in favour of her second husband, Romanus Diogenes.		7 months, 10 days.	Sons: Michael VII, CO-RULER with his mother and EMPEROR 1071-8; Andronicus; Constantine, CO-RULER with his mother and brother.	(see above).
185. ROMANUS IV Diogenes.	Date of birth unknown.	1 Jan., 1068, following his marriage to Eudocia and her abdication.	Husband of Eudocia	Deposed 19 Aug., 1071 following his defeat and capture by the Seljuks. Was released the following year, but was tortured by the Byzantines and died soon afterwards.	Injuries inflicted by torture. Age unknown.	3 years, 7 months, 18 days.	Wife: Eudocia (widow of Constantine X), EMPRESS 1067 and 1071. Stepsons: Michael VII, Andronicus and Constantine, CO-EMPERORS throughout the reign; Michael, EMPEROR 1071-8.	(See above).
186. EUDOCIA (Empress), again.	Circa 1021.	19 Aug., 1071, following the deposition of her second husband, Romanus IV.	Wife of Romanus IV, widow of Constantine X.	Deposed 24 Oct., 1071 and retired to a convent where she survived until 1096.	Natural causes, aged approx. 75.	2 months, 5 days.	Sons: Michael VII, CO-RULER with his mother, and EMPEROR 1071-8. Andronicus. Constantine.	(See above).
187. MICHAEL VII Ducas.	Exact date unknown, but was still a minor at the time of his father's death in 1067.	24 Oct., 1071, following his mother's deposition and her retirement to a convent. [Had been co-ruler with Eudocia in 1067 and again in 1071; and co-emperor with Romanus IV, 1068-71].	Son of Eudocia and Constantine X. Stepson of Romanus IV.	Deposed 24 March, 1078 and retired to the Studite monastery. Date of death unknown.	Unknown.	6 years, 5 months.	Wife: Maria (later wife of Nicephorus III). Son: Constantine Ducas (heir to the throne in the early part of Alexius I's reign). Brothers: Andronicus, CO-EMPEROR with Romanus IV, 1068-71. Constantine, CO-RULER with Eudocia in 1067 and CO-EMPEROR with Romanus IV, 1068-71. Uncle: John Ducas Caesar (grand-father of Irene, wife of Alexius I).	**Abbasid Caliphs:** al-Kaim (1031-75). **Seljuk Sultans of Rum:** Suleiman I (1077-86). **Germany:** Henry IV (1056-1106). **Popes:** Alexander II (1061-73); Gregory VII (1073-85). **Normans:** Robert Guiscard, duke of Apulia (1059-85). Roger I, count of Sicily (1072-1101).

Emperor	Born	Succeeded	Relationship to Predecessors	Died	Cause of Death, Age	Length of Reign	Relatives	Contemporary Rulers
188. NICEPHORUS III Botaniates.	Date of birth unknown.	24 March, 1078, following the deposition of Michael VII. Was proclaimed emperor 7 Jan., 1078 in opposition to Michael.	None, though he claimed descent from the family of the Phocas.	*Abdicated* 4 April, 1081 and retired to a monastery. Date of death unknown.	Unknown.	3 years and 11 days.	*Wife*: Maria (formerly wife of Michael VII). *Stepson*: Constantine Ducas.	(See above).
189. NICEPHORUS BASILACIUS	Date of birth unknown.	Rebelled against Michael VII early in 1078 in alliance with Nicephorus Bryennius. Proclaimed emperor following Bryennius' defeat by the forces of Nicephorus III.	None.	*Deposed* following his capture by the forces of Nicephorus III late spring/ early summer 1078. Subsequent fate unknown.	Unknown.	Uncertain, probably between one and two months.		(See above).
190. NICEPHORUS MELISSENUS	Date of birth unknown.	Rebelled against Nicephorus III late in 1080 and proclaimed emperor at Nicaea.	None.	*Renounced* his claim to the throne, April, 1081, in favour of his brother-in-law Alexius Comnenus. Date of death unknown.	Unknown.	Probably about 4 months.	*Brother-in-law*: Alexius I, EMPEROR 1081-1118.	(See above).
191. ALEXIUS I Comnenus.	1048.	4 April, 1081, following the abdication of Nicephorus III.	Nephew of Isaac I.	15 Aug., 1118.	Natural causes, aged 70.	37 years, 4 months, 11 days.	*Mother*: Anna Dalassena. *Wife*: Irene Dukaina (great-niece of Constantine X). *Sons*: John II, EMPEROR 1118-43. Isaac (father of Andronicus I). *Daughters*: Anna (wife of Nicephorus Bryennius). Theodora (wife of Constantine Angelus, grandmother of Isaac II and Alexius III).	**Seljuk Sultans of Rum**: Suleiman I (1077-86); Kilij Arslan I (1092-1107); Malik-Schah (1107-16); Masud I (1116-56). **Germany**: Henry IV (1056-1106); Henry V (1106-25). **Popes**: Gregory VII (1073-85); Victor III (1086-7); Urban II (1088-99); Paschal II (1099-1118). **Normans**: Robert Guiscard, duke of Apulia (1059-85); Roger I, count of Sicily (1072-1101); Simon, count of Sicily (1101-05); Roger II, count (king from 1130) of Sicily (1105-1154). CRUSADER STATES: **Jerusalem**: Godfrey of Bouillon (1099-1100); Baldwin I (1100-18). **Antioch**: Bohemund I, son of Robert Guiscard (1098-1100); Tancred, regent (1101-03); Bohemund I again (1103-04); Tancred, regent again (1104-12); Roger, regent (1112-19). **Edessa**: Baldwin I (1098-1100), later king of Jerusalem; Baldwin II (1100-18), later king of Jerusalem. **Tripoli**: Bertrand (1109-12); Pons (1112-37).

Emperor	*Born*	*Succeeded*	*Relationship to Predecessors*	*Died*	*Cause of Death, Age*	*Length of Reign*	*Relatives*	*Contemporary Rulers*
192. JOHN II Comnenus.	1088.	15 Aug., 1118.	Son of Alexius I; Great-nephew of Isaac I; Great-great-nephew of Constantine X; Cousin twice removed of Michael VII.	8 April, 1143.	Hunting accident, aged 55.	24 years, 7 months, 24 days.	*Mother*: Irene Dukaina (great-niece of Constantine X). *Wife*: Irene of Hungary. *Son*: Manuel I, EMPEROR 1143-1180. *Sister*: Anna (wife of Nicephorus Bryennius). *Nephew*: Andronicus I, EMPEROR 1183-5.	**Seljuk Sultans of Rum:** Masud I (1116-56). **Atabegs of Mosul and Aleppo:** Zangi (1127-46). **Germany:** Henry V (1106-25); Lothair II (1125-37); Conrad III (1138-52). **Popes:** Gelasius II (1118-19); Calixtus II (1119-24); Honorius II (1124-30); Innocent II (1130-43). **Normans:** Roger II, count (king from 1130) of Sicily (1105-54). **CRUSADER STATES:** **Jerusalem:** Baldwin II (1118-31); Fulk of Anjou (1131-43). **Antioch:** Roger, regent (1112-19); Baldwin II of Jerusalem, regent (1119-26); Bohemund II (1126-31); Baldwin II, regent again (1131); Fulk of Jerusalem, regent (1131-6); Raymond of Poitiers (1136-49). **Edessa:** Joscelin I (1118-31); Joscelin II (1131-44). **Tripoli:** Pons (1112-37); Raymond II (1137-52).
193. MANUEL I Comnenus.	*Circa* 1120.	8 April, 1143.	Son of John II; Grandson of Alexius I; Great-great-nephew of Isaac I; Great-great-great-nephew of Constantine X; Cousin three times removed of Michael VII.	24 Sept., 1180.	Natural causes, aged approx. 60.	37 years, 5 months, 16 days.	*Mother*: Irene of Hungary. *Wife*: Mary of Antioch. *Son*: Alexius II, EMPEROR 1180-83. *Cousin*: Andronicus I, EMPEROR 1183-5.	**Seljuk Sultans of Rum:** Masud I (1116-56); Kilij Arslan II (1156-92). **Atabegs of Aleppo:** Zangi (1127-46); Nureddin (1146-74). **Ayyubid Sultans:** Saladin (1174-93). **Serbia:** Stephen Nemanja (c. 1167-96). **Germany:** Conrad III (1138-52); Frederick I, Barbarossa (1152-90). **Popes:** Celestine II (1143-4); Lucius II (1144-5); Eugenius III (1145-53); Anastasius IV (1153-4); Adrian IV (1154-9); Alexander III (1159-81). **Normans:** Roger II, count (king from 1130) of Sicily (1105-54); William I (1154-66); William II (1166-89). **CRUSADER STATES:** **Jerusalem:** Baldwin III (1143-63); Amalric I (1163-74); Baldwin IV (1174-85). **Antioch:** Raymond of Poitiers (1136-49); Raynald of Chatillon (1153-60); Bohemund III (1163-1201). **Edessa:** Joscelin II (1131-44). **Tripoli:** Raymond II (1137-52); Raymond III (1152-87).
194. ALEXIUS II Comnenus.	1169.	24 Sept., 1180.	Son of Manuel I; Grandson of John II; Great-grandson of Alexius I; Great-great-great-nephew of Isaac I; Great-great-great-great-nephew of Constantine X; Cousin four times removed of Michael VII.	Sept., 1183.	Strangled on the orders of Andronicus I. Age 14.	Approx. 3 years.	*Mother*: Mary of Antioch. *Wife*: Agnes-Anna (later wife of Andronicus I). *Cousin once removed*: Andronicus I, EMPEROR 1183-5.	**Popes:** Alexander III (1159-81); Lucius III (1181-5). (Otherwise see above).

Emperor	Born	Succeeded	Relationship to Predecessors	Died	Cause of Death, Age	Length of Reign	Relatives	Contemporary Rulers
195. ANDRONICUS I Comnenus.	Exact date uncertain, but probably between 1110 and 1120.	Crowned co-emperor with Alexius II, Sept., 1183, soon after which Alexius was murdered.	Cousin once removed of Alexius II; Cousin of Manuel I; Nephew of John II; Grandson of Alexius I; Great-great-nephew of Isaac I; Great-great-great-nephew of Constantine X; Cousin three times removed of Michael VII.	12 Sept., 1185.	Killed by the mob. Probably aged about 70.	Approx. 2 years.	*Father*: Isaac (son of Alexius I). *Wife*: Agnes-Anna (formerly wife of Alexius II). *Grandson*: Alexius I, Emperor of Trebizond 1204-22. *Cousins once removed*: Isaac II, EMPEROR 1185-95 and 1203-4. Alexius III, EMPEROR 1195-1203.	(See above).
196. ISAAC COMNENUS of Cyprus.	Date of birth unknown.	Rebelled against Andronicus I in 1184 and became the independent ruler of Cyprus.	Cousin twice removed of Andronicus I; Cousin once removed of Alexius II; Great-nephew of Manuel I, etc., etc.	*Deposed* 1191 by Richard I of England, and imprisoned. Date of death unknown.	Unknown.	Approx. 7 years.		(See above and below.)

Emperor	Born	Succeeded	Relationship to Predecessors	Died	Cause of Death, Age	Length of Reign	Relatives	Contemporary Rulers
197. ISAAC II Angelus.	Circa 1155.	12 Sept., 1185, following the downfall of Andronicus I.	Great-grandson of Alexius I, etc., etc.	Deposed 8 April, 1195, blinded and imprisoned. Later restored to the throne in association with his son Alexius IV, but again deposed, 28 Jan., 1204, and died soon afterwards.	Probably shock, following the murder of his son, Alexius IV. Age approx. 49.	9 years, 6 months, 27 days.	Grandfather: Constantine Angelus. Grandmother: Theodora Comnena (daughter of Alexius I). Son: Alexius IV, EMPEROR 1203-4. Brother: Alexius III, EMPEROR 1195-1203.	Seljuk Sultans of Rum: Kilij Arslan II (1156-92); Kaikosru I (1192-6). Ayyubid Sultans: Saladin (1174-93); al-Aziz (1193-9). Bulgaria: Asen I (1187-96). Serbia: Stephen Nemanja (c. 1167-96). Germany: Frederick I, Barbarossa (1152-90); Henry VI (1190-97). Popes: Urban III (1185-7); Gregory VIII (1187); Clement III (1187-91); Celestine III (1191-8). Normans: William II, king of Sicily (1166-89); Tancred (1190-94): Sicily then united with the German kingdom under Henry VI. CRUSADER STATES: Jerusalem: Baldwin V (1185-6); Guy of Lusignan (1186-92); Conrad of Montferrat (1192); Henry of Champagne (1192-7). Antioch: Bohemund III (1163-1201). Tripoli: Raymond III (1152-87); Bohemund, later IV of Antioch (1187-1233).
198. ALEXIUS III Angelus-Comnenus.	Date of birth unknown, but older than his brother Isaac II, so born before circa 1155.	8 April, 1195, having deposed his brother Isaac II.	Brother of Isaac II; Great-grandson of Alexius I etc., etc.	Deposed following his flight from Constantinople 17 July, 1203. Later unsuccessfully rebelled against Theodore I Lascaris and was confined to a monastery where he died circa 1211.	Unknown.	8 years, 3 months, 9 days.	Grandfather: Constantine Angelus. Grandmother: Theodora Comnena (daughter of Alexius I). Daughters: Irene (grandmother of Michael VIII). Anna (wife of Theodore I). Eudocia (wife of Alexius V). Nephew: Alexius IV, EMPEROR 1203-4.	Seljuk Sultans of Rum: Kaikosru I (1192-6); Suleiman II (1196-1204). Ayyubid Sultans: al-Aziz (1193-9); al-Adil I (1199-1218). Bulgaria: Asen I (1187-96); Peter (1196-7); Kalojan (1197-1207). Serbia: Stephen Nemanja (c. 1167-96); Stephen the First-Crowned (1196-c. 1228). Germany: Henry VI (1190-97); Otto IV (1198-1212). Popes: Celestine III (1191-8); Innocent III (1198-1216). Sicily: Henry VI of Germany (1194-7); Frederick II, later king of Germany (1198-1250). CRUSADER STATES: Jerusalem: Henry of Champagne (1192-7); Amalric II (1198-1205). Antioch: Bohemund III (1163-1201); Bohemund IV (1201-33). Tripoli: Bohemund, later IV of Antioch (1187-1233).
199. ALEXIUS IV Angelus.	Date of birth unknown.	Established as a puppet-ruler by the forces of the Fourth Crusade, 18 July, 1203, following the flight of Alexius III.	Nephew of Alexius III; Son of Isaac II; Great-great-grandson of Alexius I, etc., etc.	28 Jan., 1204.	Strangled on the orders of Alexius V. Age unknown.	6 months, 10 days.	Father: Isaac II, formerly EMPEROR (1185-95), and CO-EMPEROR throughout Alexius IV's reign.	(See above).

Emperor	Born	Succeeded	Relationship to Predecessors	Died	Cause of Death, Age	Length of Reign	Relatives	Contemporary Rulers
200. ALEXIUS V Ducas Murtzuphlus.	Date of birth unknown.	5 Feb., 1204, soon after the assassination of Alexius IV	Son-in-law of Alexius III.	Deposed following his flight from Constantinople 12 April, 1204. Sought refuge with his father-in-law, but the former Alexius III blinded him. Soon afterwards he was captured and killed by the Crusaders.	Thrown from the top of a column in Constantinople. Age unknown.	2 months, 7 days.	Wife: Eudocia (daughter of Alexius III).	Empire of Trebizond: Alexius I Comnenus, grandson of Andronicus I, great-great-grandson of Alexius I (1204-22). (Otherwise see above).
201. THEODORE I Comnenus Lascaris, **Emperor of Nicaea.**	Circa 1175.	Established the Empire of Nicaea after the fall of Constantinople to the crusaders in 1204, but was not crowned until 1208.	Son-in-law of Alexius III.	1222.	Natural causes, aged approx. 47.	Approx. 14 years from his coronation.	Wife: Anna Angelina (daughter of Alexius III). Daughter: Irene (wife of John III). Grandson: Theodore II, EMPEROR OF NICAEA 1254-8.	Latin Empire of Constantinople: Baldwin I of Flanders (1204-5); Henry of Flanders (1206-16); Peter of Courtenay (1217); Yolande (1217-19); Robert of Courtenay (1221-8). Despotate of Epirus: Michael I (1204-c. 1215); Theodore (c. 1215-1224). Empire of Trebizond: Alexius I (1204-22). Seljuk Sultans of Rum: Kilij Arslan III (1204); Kaikosru I, again (1204-10); Kaikaus I (1210-20); Kaikubad I (1220-37). Ayyubid Sultans: al-Adil I (1199-1218); al-Kamil I (1218-38). Bulgaria: Kalojan (1197-1207); Boril (1207-18); Ivan Asen II (1218-41). Serbia: Stephen the First-Crowned (1196-c. 1228). Germany: Otto IV (1198-1212); Frederick II (1212-1250). Popes: Innocent III (1198-1216); Honorius III (1216-27). Sicily: Frederick II, king of Germany from 1212 (1198-1250). CRUSADER STATES: Jerusalem: Amalric II (1198-1205); Mary (1205-10); John of Brienne (1210-1225). Antioch: Bohemund IV (1201-33), also count of Tripoli.
202. JOHN III Ducas-Vatatzes, **Emperor of Nicaea.**	1192.	1222.	Son-in-law of Theodore I.	3 Nov., 1254.	Natural causes, aged 62.	Approx. 32 years.	Wife: Irene (daughter of Theodore I). Son: Theodore II, EMPEROR OF NICAEA 1254-8. Grandson: John IV, EMPEROR OF NICAEA 1258-61.	Latin Empire of Constantinople: Robert of Courtenay (1221-8); Baldwin II (1228-61). Despotate of Epirus: Theodore (c. 1215-1224); Michael II (c. 1237-1271). Empire of Thessalonica: Theodore, formerly despot of Epirus (1224-30); Manuel (1230-37); John (1237-42). Despotate of Thessalonica: John, formerly emperor (1242-4); Demetrius (1244-6). Empire of Trebizond: Andronicus I (1222-35); John I (1235-8); Manuel I (1238-63). Seljuk Sultans of Rum: Kaikubad I (1220-37); Kaikosru II (1237-45); Kaikaus II (1246-57); Kilij Arslan IV (1248-65); Kaikubad II (1249-57).

Emperor	Born	Succeeded	Relationship to Predecessors	Died	Cause of Death, Age	Length of Reign	Relatives	Contemporary Rulers
202. JOHN III (continued).								**Ayyubid Sultans:** al-Kamil I (1218-38). **Bulgaria:** Ivan Asen II (1218-41); Koloman Asen (1241-6); Michael Asen (1246-56). **Serbia:** Stephen the First-Crowned (1196-*c.*1228); Stephen Radoslav (*c.*1228-*c.*1233); Stephen Vladislav (*c.*1233-1242); Stephen Uros I (1242-76). **Germany:** Frederick II (1212-50); Conrad IV (1250-54). **Popes:** Honorius III (1216-27); Gregory IX (1227-41); Celestine IV (1241); Innocent IV (1243-54). **Sicily:** Frederick II of Germany (1198-1250); Conrad IV of Germany (1250-54). **CRUSADER STATES:** **Jerusalem:** John of Brienne (1210-25); Frederick II of Germany (1225-43); Conrad, later IV of Germany (1243-4). **Antioch:** Bohemund IV (1201-33); Bohemund V (1233-52); Bohemund VI (1252-68): also counts of **Tripoli.**
203. THEODORE II Ducas-Lascaris, **Emperor of Nicaea.** 	1222.	3 Nov., 1254.	Son of John III; Grandson of Theodore I; Great-grandson of Alexius III; Great-great-great-great-grandson of Alexius I.	Aug., 1258.	Natural causes, aged 36.	3¾ years.	*Mother:* Irene (daughter of Theodore I and Anna Angelina). *Wife:* Helena (daughter of Ivan Asen II of Bulgaria). *Son:* John IV, EMPEROR OF NICAEA 1258-61. *Daughters:* Irene (wife of Constantine Tich of Bulgaria). Maria (wife of Nicephorus I of Epirus).	**Latin Empire of Constantinople:** Baldwin II (1228-61). **Despotate of Epirus:** Michael II (*c.*1237-71). **Empire of Trebizond:** Manuel I (1238-63). **Seljuk Sultans of Rum:** Kaikaus II (1246-57); Kilij Arslan IV (1248-65); Kaikubad II (1249-57). **Bulgaria:** Michael Asen (1246-56); Constantine Tich (1257-77). **Serbia:** Stephen Uros I (1242-76). **Popes:** Alexander IV (1254-61). **Sicily:** Manfred (1254-66, crowned in 1258). **CRUSADER STATES:** **Antioch:** Bohemund VI (1252-68), also count of **Tripoli.**
204. JOHN IV Lascaris, **Emperor of Nicaea.**	Circa 1250.	Aug., 1258.	Son of Theodore II; Grandson of John III; Great-grandson of Theodore I; Great-great-grandson of Alexius III; Great-great-great-great-great-grandson of Alexius I.	*Deposed* after the recapture of Constantinople in July 1261, and blinded and imprisoned before the end of the year. Died *circa* 1300.	Probably natural causes. Age approx. 50.	Approx. 3 years.	*Mother:* Helena (daughter of Ivan Asen II of Bulgaria). *Sisters:* Irene (wife of Constantine Tich of Bulgaria). Maria (wife of Nicephorus I of Epirus).	(See above).

THE PALAEOLOGAN DYNASTY

Emperor	Born	Succeeded	Relationship to Predecessors	Died	Cause of Death, Age	Length of Reign	Relatives	Contemporary Rulers
205. MICHAEL VIII Palaeologus, **Emperor of Nicaea** 1258-61 and of the restored Byzantine Empire 1261-82.	Circa 1225.	Crowned co-emperor with John IV in Dec., 1258. Re-crowned as sole emperor in Constantinople, 15 Aug., 1261.	Great-grandson of Alexius III; Great-great-great-great-grandson of Alexius I.	11 Dec., 1282.	Natural causes, aged approx. 57.	2 years, 8 months (in Nicaea). 21 years, 3 months, 26 days (in Constantinople).	*Grandmother*: Irene (daughter of Alexius III). *Wife*: Theodora. *Son*: Andronicus II, EMPEROR 1282-1328. *Grandson*: Michael IX, CO-EMPEROR 1295-1320.	**Latin Empire of Constantinople:** Baldwin II (1228-61). **Despotate of Epirus:** Michael II (c. 1237-1271); Nicephorus I (1271-96). **Sebastocrators of Thessaly:** John I (1271-96). **Empire of Trebizond:** Manuel I (1238-63); Andronicus II (1263-6); George (1266-80); John II (1280-97). **Seljuk Sultans of Rum:** Kilij Arslan IV (1248-65); Kaikosru III (1265-82). **Bulgaria:** Constantine Tich (1257-77); Ivajlo (1278-9); Ivan Asen III (1279-80); George I Terter (1280-92). **Serbia:** Stephen Uros I (1242-76); Stephen Dragutin (1276-82). **Popes:** Alexander IV (1254-61); Urban IV (1261-4); Clement IV (1265-8); Gregory X (1271-6); Innocent V (1276); Adrian V (1276); John XXI (1276-7); Nicholas III (1277-80); Martin IV (1281-5). **Sicily:** Manfred (1254-66, crowned in 1258); Charles of Anjou (1266-82). **CRUSADER STATES:** **Antioch:** Bohemund VI (1252-68). **Tripoli:** Bohemund VI of Antioch (ruler of both states 1252-68, and of Tripoli alone 1268-75); Bohemund VII (1275-87).
206. ANDRONICUS II Palaeologus.	1258.	11 Dec., 1282. [Had been co-emperor with Michael VIII from 1272].	Son of Michael VIII, *etc., etc.*	*Abdicated* 24 May, 1328 and retired to a monastery. Died Feb. 13, 1332.	Natural causes, aged 74.	45 years, 5 months, 13 days.	*Wife*: Anna of Hungary. *Son*: Michael IX, CO-EMPEROR 21 May, 1295-12 Oct., 1320. *Grandson*: Andronicus III, son of Michael IX, EMPEROR 1328-41.	**Despotate of Epirus:** Nicephorus I (1271-96); Thomas (1296-1318); Nicholas Orsini (1318-23); John Orsini (1323-35). **Sebastocrators of Thessaly:** John I (1271-96); Constantine (1296-1303); John II (1303-18). **Empire of Trebizond:** John II (1280-97); Alexius II (1297-1330). **Seljuk Sultans of Rum:** Masud II (1282-1304); Kaikubad III (1284-1307); Masud III (1307-8). **Ottoman Sultans:** Osman (1288-1326); Orchan (1326-62). **Bulgaria:** George I Terter (1280-92); Smiletz (1292-8); (*Interregnum* 1298-1300); Caka (1300); Theodore Svetoslav (1300-22); George II Terter (1322-3); Michael Sisman (1323-30). **Serbia:** Stephen Uros II (1282-1321); Stephen Uros III (1321-31). **Popes:** Martin IV (1281-5); Honorius IV (1285-7); Nicholas IV (1288-92); Celestine V (1294); Boniface VIII (1294-1303); Benedict XI (1303-4); Clement V (1305-14); John XXII (1316-34). **CRUSADER STATES:** **Tripoli:** Bohemund VII (1275-87); Lucia (1288-9).

Emperor	Born	Succeeded	Relationship to Predecessors	Died	Cause of Death, Age	Length of Reign	Relatives	Contemporary Rulers
207. ANDRONICUS III, Palaeologus.	1296.	24 May, 1328, following the abdication of Andronicus II. [Had been co-emperor with Andronicus II from 2 Feb., 1325].	Son of Michael IX; Grandson of Andronicus II; Great-grandson of Michael VIII, *etc., etc.*	15 June, 1341.	Natural causes, aged 45.	13 years, and 22 days.	*Mother*: Maria (Xene) of Armenia. *Wife*: Anne of Savoy. *Son*: John V, EMPEROR 1341-91.	**Despotate of Epirus:** John Orsini (1323-35); Nicephorus II (1335-40). **Empire of Trebizond:** Alexius II (1297-1330); Andronicus III (1330-32); Manuel II (1332); Basil (1332-40); Irene, Anna (1340-42). **Ottoman Sultans:** Orchan (1326-62). **Bulgaria:** Michael Sisman (1323-30); Ivan Stephen (1330-31); Ivan Alexander (1331-71). **Serbia:** Stephen Uros III (1321-31); Stephen Dusan (1331-55). **Popes:** John XXII (1316-34); Benedict XII (1334-42).
208. JOHN V Palaeologus.	18 April, 1332.	15 June, 1341.	Son of Andronicus III; Grandson of Michael IX; Great-grandson of Andronicus II; Great-great-grandson of Michael VIII, *etc., etc.*	16 Feb., 1391.	Natural causes, aged 59.	49 years, 8 months, 1 day.	*Mother*: Anne of Savoy. *Wife*: Helena (daughter of John VI). *Sons*: Andronicus IV, RIVAL EMPEROR 1376-9; Manuel II, EMPEROR 1391-1423. *Grandson*: John VII, RIVAL EMPEROR 1390.	**Empire of Trebizond:** Irene, Anna (1340-42); John III (1342-4); Michael (1344-9); Alexius III (1349-90); Manuel III (1390-1417). **Ottoman Sultans:** Orchan (1326-62); Murad I (1362-89); Bajezid I (1389-1402). **Bulgaria:** Ivan Alexander (1331-71); Ivan Sisman (1371-93). **Serbia:** Stephen Dusan (1331-55); Czar Stephen Uros (1355-71); Prince Lazar (1371-89); Stephen Lazarevic (1389-1427). **Popes:** Benedict XII (1334-42); Clement VI (1342-52); Innocent VI (1352-62); Urban V (1362-70); Gregory XI (1370-78); Urban VI (1378-89); Boniface IX (1389-1404).
209. JOHN VI Cantacuzenus.	*Circa* 1292.	Crowned co-emperor with John V, 13 May, 1347, and temporarily deposed his younger colleague in April, 1353.	None.	*Deposed* 22 Nov., 1354 and retired to a monastery where he survived until 15 June, 1383.	Natural causes, aged approx. 91.	Approx. 5 years and 11 months (with John V); Approx. 1 year and 7 months (alone).	*Wife*: Irene (great-grand-daughter of Michael VIII). *Sons:* Matthew, CO-EMPEROR with his father from Feb., 1354. Manuel, despot of the Morea. *Daughters:* Theodora (wife of the Ottoman sultan Orchan). Helena (wife of John V). *Grandsons:* Andronicus IV, EMPEROR 1376-9. Manuel II, EMPEROR 1391-1423. *Great-grandson:* John VII, EMPEROR 1390.	(See above).

Emperor	Born	Succeeded	Relationship to Predecessors	Died	Cause of Death, Age	Length of Reign	Relatives	Contemporary Rulers
210. ANDRONICUS IV, Palaeologus.	*Circa* 1348.	Rebelled against John V and took possession of Constantinople 12 Aug., 1376.	Son of John V; Grandson of Andronicus III and of John VI; Great-grandson of Michael IX; Great-great-grandson of Andronicus II; Great-great-great-grandson of Michael VIII, *etc., etc.*	*Deposed* 1 July, 1379 by his father, John V, and brother, Manuel II. Died in 1385.	Presumably, natural causes. Age approx. 37.	2 years, 10 months, 19 days.	*Mother*: Helena (daughter of John VI). *Wife*: Maria (daughter of Ivan Alexander of Bulgaria). *Son*: John VII, EMPEROR 1390. *Brother*: Manuel II, EMPEROR 1391-1423. *Uncle*: Matthew, CO-EMPEROR in 1354 with John VI.	(See above).
211. JOHN VII Palaeologus.	*Circa* 1370.	Rebelled against John V and took possession of Constantinople, 14 April, 1390.	Son of Andronicus IV; Grandson of John V; Great-grandson of Andronicus III and of John VI; Great-great-grandson of Michael IX; Great-great-great-grandson of Andronicus II; Great-great-great-great-grandson of Michael VIII, *etc., etc.*	*Deposed* 17 Sept., 1390. Later acted as regent for his uncle Manuel II during the latter's absence in Western Europe, 1399-1402. Died 22 Sept., 1408.	Presumably, natural causes. Age approx. 38.	5 months, 3 days.	*Mother*: Maria (daughter of Ivan Alexander of Bulgaria). *Uncle*: Manuel II, EMPEROR 1391-1423. *Cousins*: John VIII, EMPEROR 1423-48. Constantine XI, EMPEROR 1448-53.	(See above).
212. MANUEL II Palaeologus.	1350.	16 Feb., 1391. [Had been co-emperor with John V from 25 Sept, 1373].	Son of John V, *etc.* (Same as Andronicus IV —see above).	*Abdicated* in 1423 and retired to a monastery where he died 21 July, 1425.	Natural causes, aged 75.	Approx. 32 years.	*Mother*: Helena (daughter of John VI). *Wife*: Helena Dragas. *Sons*: John VIII, EMPEROR 1423-48. Constantine XI, EMPEROR 1448-53. *Brother*: Andronicus IV, RIVAL EMPEROR 1376-9. *Nephew*: John VII, RIVAL EMPEROR 1390, and regent 1399-1402 during Manuel's absence in Western Europe. *Uncle*: Matthew, CO-EMPEROR in 1354 with John VI.	**Empire of Trebizond**: Manuel III (1390-1417); Alexius IV (1417-46). **Ottoman Sultans**: Bajezid I (1389-1402); Muhammed I (1402-21); Suleiman (1402-10); Musa (1411-13); Murad II (1421-51). **Bulgaria**: Ivan Sisman (1371-93). **Serbia**: Stephen Lazarevic (1389-1427). **Popes**: Boniface IX (1389-1404); Innocent VII (1404-6); Gregory XII (1406-15); Martin V (1417-31).

Emperor	Born	Succeeded	Relationship to Predecessors	Died	Cause of Death, Age	Length of Reign	Relatives	Contemporary Rulers
213. JOHN VIII Palaeologus.	1392.	1423, following the abdication of Manuel II. [Had been co-emperor with his father from 19 Jan., 1421].	Son of Manuel II; Grandson of John V; Great-grandson of Andronicus III and of John VI; Great-great-grandson of Michael IX; Great-great-great-grandson of Andronicus II; Great-great-great-great-grandson of Michael VIII, etc., etc.	31 Oct., 1448.	Natural causes, aged 56.	Approx. 25 years.	*Mother*: Helena Dragas. *Brother*: Constantine XI, EMPEROR 1448-53. *Uncle*: Andronicus IV, EMPEROR 1376-9. *Cousin*: John VII, EMPEROR 1390.	**Empire of Trebizond:** Alexius IV (1417-46); John IV (1446-58). **Ottoman Sultans:** Murad II (1421-51). **Serbia:** Stephen Lazarevic (1389-1427); George Brankovic (1427-56). **Popes:** Martin V (1417-31); Eugenius IV (1431-47); Nicholas V (1447-55).
214. CONSTANTINE XI, Palaeologus.	1404.	31 Oct., 1448.	Brother of John VIII; Son of Manuel II, *etc.* (Same as John VIII – see above).	29 May, 1453.	Killed in battle, defending the walls of Constantinople against the Turkish conquerors. Age 49.	4 years, 6 months, 29 days.	*Mother*: Helena Dragas. *Wife*: Magdalena. *Uncle*: Andronicus IV, EMPEROR 1376-9. *Cousin*: John VII, EMPEROR 1390.	**Empire of Trebizond:** John IV (1446-58). **Ottoman Sultans:** Murad II (1421-51); Muhammed II the Conqueror (1451-81). **Serbia:** George Brankovic (1427-56). **Popes:** Nicholas V (1447-55).

THE HERACLIAN DYNASTY

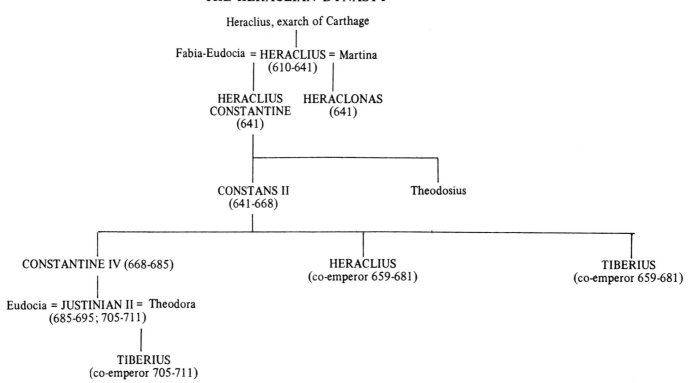

Heraclius, exarch of Carthage

Fabia-Eudocia = HERACLIUS = Martina
(610-641)

HERACLIUS   HERACLONAS
CONSTANTINE   (641)
(641)

CONSTANS II   Theodosius
(641-668)

CONSTANTINE IV (668-685)   HERACLIUS   TIBERIUS
(co-emperor 659-681)   (co-emperor 659-681)

Eudocia = JUSTINIAN II = Theodora
(685-695; 705-711)

TIBERIUS
(co-emperor 705-711)

THE SYRIAN DYNASTY

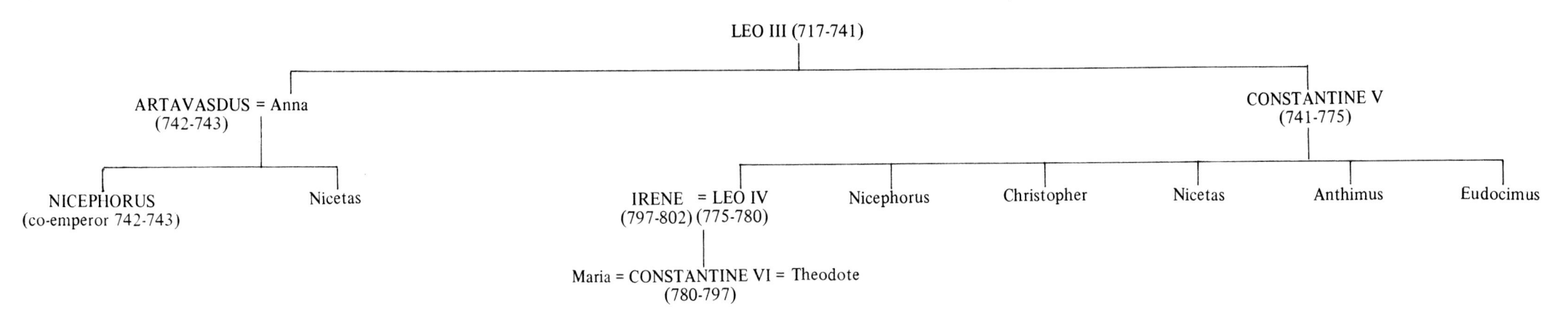

LEO III (717-741)

ARTAVASDUS = Anna
(742-743)

CONSTANTINE V
(741-775)

NICEPHORUS
(co-emperor 742-743)

Nicetas

IRENE = LEO IV
(797-802) (775-780)

Nicephorus   Christopher   Nicetas   Anthimus   Eudocimus

Maria = CONSTANTINE VI = Theodote
(780-797)

THE AMORIAN DYNASTY

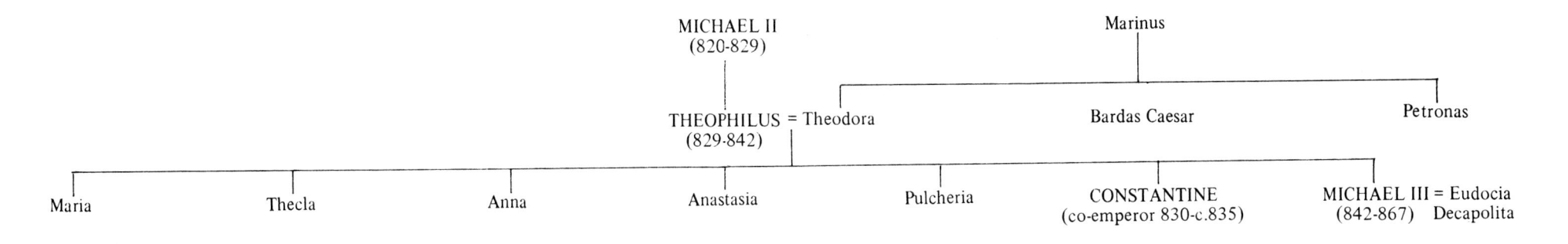

MICHAEL II
(820-829)

Marinus

THEOPHILUS = Theodora
(829-842)

Bardas Caesar

Petronas

Maria   Thecla   Anna   Anastasia   Pulcheria   CONSTANTINE
(co-emperor 830-c.835)

MICHAEL III = Eudocia
(842-867) Decapolita

THE MACEDONIAN DYNASTY

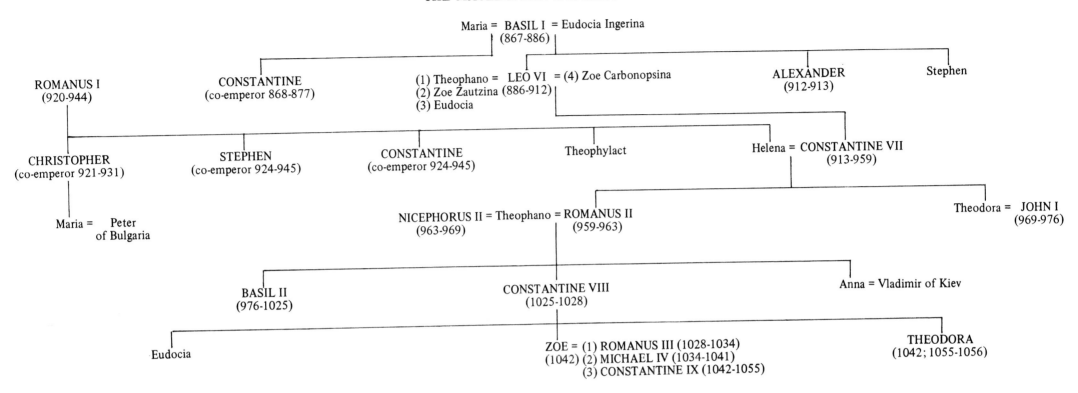

Maria = BASIL I = Eudocia Ingerina
(867-886)

ROMANUS I
(920-944)

CONSTANTINE
(co-emperor 868-877)

(1) Theophano = LEO VI = (4) Zoe Carbonopsina
(2) Zoe Zautzina (886-912)
(3) Eudocia

ALEXANDER
(912-913)

Stephen

CHRISTOPHER
(co-emperor 921-931)

STEPHEN
(co-emperor 924-945)

CONSTANTINE
(co-emperor 924-945)

Theophylact

Helena = CONSTANTINE VII
(913-959)

Theodora = JOHN I
(969-976)

Maria = Peter
of Bulgaria

NICEPHORUS II = Theophano = ROMANUS II
(963-969)   (959-963)

BASIL II
(976-1025)

CONSTANTINE VIII
(1025-1028)

Anna = Vladimir of Kiev

Eudocia

ZOE = (1) ROMANUS III (1028-1034)
(1042) (2) MICHAEL IV (1034-1041)
         (3) CONSTANTINE IX (1042-1055)

THEODORA
(1042; 1055-1056)

THE DYNASTIES OF THE DUCAS AND THE COMNENI

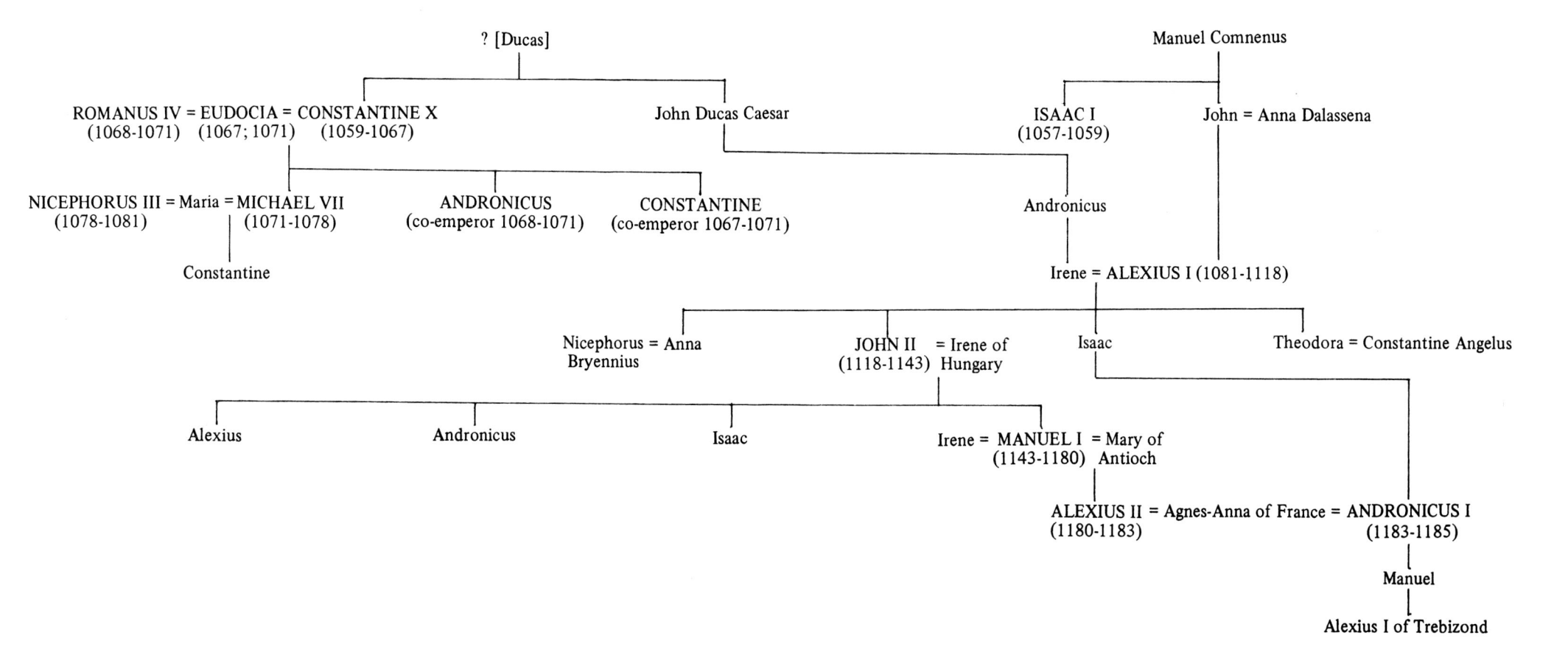

THE DYNASTIES OF THE ANGELI AND THE LASCARIDS

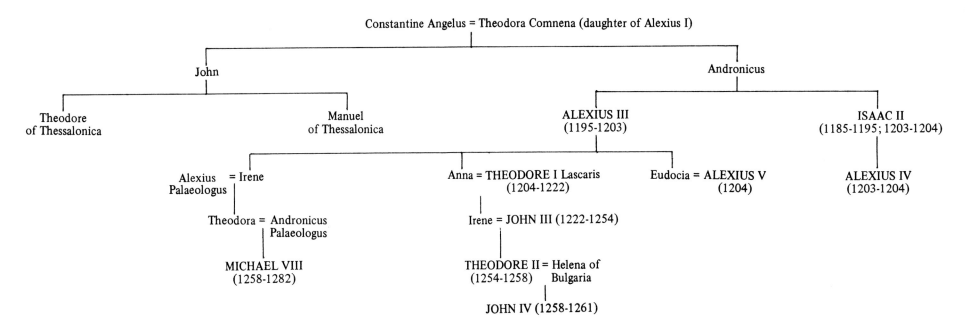

Constantine Angelus = Theodora Comnena (daughter of Alexius I)

John

Andronicus

Theodore
of Thessalonica

Manuel
of Thessalonica

ALEXIUS III
(1195-1203)

ISAAC II
(1185-1195; 1203-1204)

Alexius = Irene
Palaeologus

Anna = THEODORE I Lascaris
(1204-1222)

Eudocia = ALEXIUS V
(1204)

ALEXIUS IV
(1203-1204)

Theodora = Andronicus
Palaeologus

Irene = JOHN III (1222-1254)

MICHAEL VIII
(1258-1282)

THEODORE II = Helena of
(1254-1258)   Bulgaria

JOHN IV (1258-1261)

THE PALAEOLOGAN DYNASTY

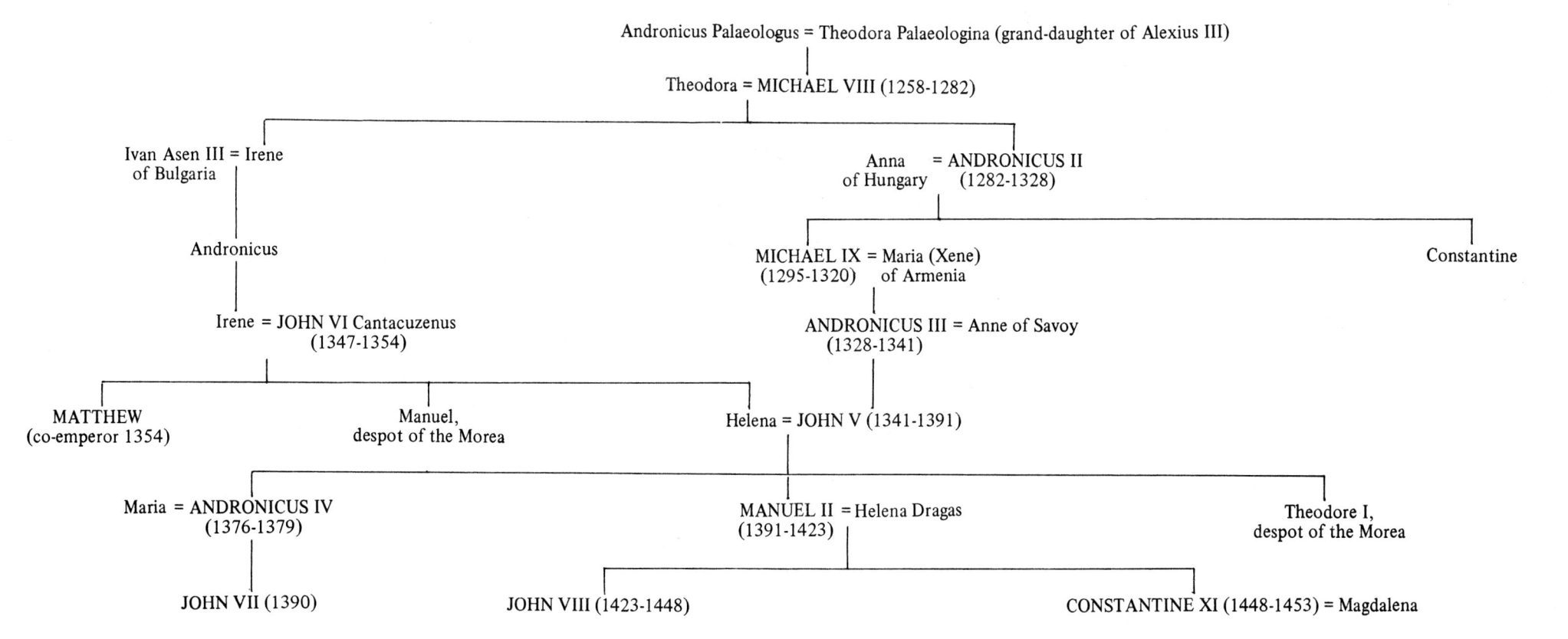

Andronicus Palaeologus = Theodora Palaeologina (grand-daughter of Alexius III)

Theodora = MICHAEL VIII (1258-1282)

Ivan Asen III = Irene
of Bulgaria

Anna   = ANDRONICUS II
of Hungary   (1282-1328)

Andronicus

MICHAEL IX = Maria (Xene)
(1295-1320)   of Armenia

Constantine

Irene = JOHN VI Cantacuzenus
(1347-1354)

ANDRONICUS III = Anne of Savoy
(1328-1341)

MATTHEW
(co-emperor 1354)

Manuel,
despot of the Morea

Helena = JOHN V (1341-1391)

Maria = ANDRONICUS IV
(1376-1379)

MANUEL II = Helena Dragas
(1391-1423)

Theodore I,
despot of the Morea

JOHN VII (1390)

JOHN VIII (1423-1448)

CONSTANTINE XI (1448-1453) = Magdalena

THE CHRONOLOGICAL SEQUENCE

OF THE BYZANTINE EMPERORS,

A.D. 491–1453.

Anastasius I .... A.D. 491-518
Justin I 518-527
Justin I and Justinian I 527
Justinian I 527-565
Justin II 565-578
Justin II and Tiberius II 578
Justin II and Tiberius II 578-582
Tiberius II 582-c.589
Maurice Tiberius 582-c.589
Maurice Tiberius and Theodosius c.589-602
Phocas 602-608
Phocas and Heraclius (in revolt) 608-610
Heraclius 610-613
Heraclius and Heraclius Constantine 613-638
Heraclius, Heraclius Constantine
              and Heraclonas 638-641
Heraclius Constantine and Heraclonas 641
Heraclonas 641
Heraclonas and Constans II 641
Constans II (i.e. Constantine III) 641-654
Constans II and Constantine IV 654-659
Constans II, Constantine IV,
              Heraclius and Tiberius 659-668
Constantine IV, Heraclius and Tiberius 668-681
Constantine IV 681-685
Justinian II 685-695
Leontius 695-698
Tiberius III 698-705
Justinian II (again) 705
Justinian II and Tiberius 705-711
Philippicus 711-713
Anastasius II 713-715
Theodosius III 715-717
Theodosius III and Leo III (in revolt) 717
Leo III 717-720
Leo III and Constantine V 720-741
Constantine V 741-742
Constantine V and Artavasdus (in revolt) 742
Constantine V and Artavasdus
              with Nicephorus (in revolt) 742-743

Constantine V 743-751
Constantine V and Leo IV 751-775
Leo IV 775-776
Leo IV and Constantine VI 776-780
Constantine VI and Irene 780-797
Irene 797-802
Nicephorus I 802-803
Nicephorus I and Stauracius 803-811
Stauracius 811
Michael I 811
Michael I and Theophylactus 811-813
Leo V 813
Leo V and Constantine 813-820
Michael II 820-821
Michael II and Theophilus 821-829
Theophilus 829-830
Theophilus and Constantine 830-c.835
Theophilus c.835-840
Theophilus and Michael III 840-842
Michael III 842-866
Michael III and Basil I 866-867
Basil I 867-868
Basil I and Constantine 868-870
Basil I, Constantine and Leo VI 870-877
Basil I, Leo VI and Alexander 877-886
Leo VI and Alexander 886-908
Leo VI, Alexander and Constantine VII .. 908-912
Alexander and Constantine VII 912-913
Constantine VII 913-920
Constantine VII and Romanus I 920-921
Constantine VII, Romanus I
              and Christopher 921-924
Constantine VII, Romanus I, Christopher,
              Stephen and Constantine 924-931
Constantine VII, Romanus I,
              Stephen and Constantine 931-944
Constantine VII, Stephen and Constantine 944-945
Constantine VII 945
Constantine VII and Romanus II 945-959

Romanus II 959-960
Romanus II and Basil II 960-961
Romanus II, Basil II and Constantine VIII 961-963
Basil II and Constantine VIII
              (with Theophano as regent) 963
Nicephorus II, Basil II and
              Constantine VIII 963-969
John I, Basil II and Constantine VIII 969-976
Basil II and Constantine VIII 976-1025
Constantine VIII 1025-1028
Romanus III 1028-1034
Michael IV 1034-1041
Michael V 1041-1042
Zoe and Theodora 1042
Constantine IX 1042-1055
Theodora (again) 1055-1056
Michael VI 1056-1057
Isaac I 1057-1059
Constantine X 1059-1067
Eudocia, Michael VII and Constantine 1067
Romanus IV, Michael VII,
              Andronicus and Constantine 1068-1071
Eudocia (again) and Michael VII 1071
Michael VII 1071-1078
Michael VII and Nicephorus III (in revolt) 1078
Nicephorus III 1078
Nicephorus III and
              Nicephorus Basilacius (in revolt) 1078
Nicephorus III 1078-1080
Nicephorus III and
              Nicephorus Melissenus (in revolt) 1080-1081
Alexius I 1081-1118
John II 1118-1143
Manuel I 1143-1180
Alexius II 1180-1183
Alexius II and Andronicus I 1183
Andronicus I 1183-1184
Andronicus I and
              Isaac Comnenus of Cyprus (in revolt) 1184-1185

Isaac II and
              Isaac Comnenus of Cyprus (in revolt) 1185-1191
Isaac II 1191-1195
Alexius III 1195-1203
Isaac II (again) and Alexius IV 1203-1204
Alexius V 1204
Theodore I of Nicaea ..1204 (crowned 1208)-1222
John III of Nicaea 1222-1254
Theodore II of Nicaea 1254-1258
John IV of Nicaea 1258
John IV and Michael VIII of Nicaea 1258-1261
Michael VIII 1261-1272
Michael VIII and Andronicus II 1272-1282
Andronicus II 1282-1295
Andronicus II and Michael IX 1295-1320
Andronicus II 1320-1325
Andronicus II and Andronicus III 1325-1328
Andronicus III 1328-1341
John V 1341-1347
John V and John VI 1347-1353
John VI 1353-1354
John VI and Matthew 1354
John V (restored) 1354-1373
John V and Manuel II 1373-1376
John V and Manuel II,
              Andronicus IV (in revolt) 1376-1379
John V and Manuel II 1379-1390
John V and Manuel II, John VII (in revolt).... 1390
John V and Manuel II 1390-1391
Manuel II 1391-1399
Manuel II and John VII (as regent) 1399-1402
Manuel II 1402-1421
Manuel II and John VIII 1421-1423
John VIII 1423-1448
Constantine XI 1448-1453